HACK
YOUR
HOME

HACK YOUR YOUR HOME

Clean, declutter and style
to create a space you love!

Tanya Mukendi

Thorsons

Thorsons
An imprint of HarperCollins*Publishers*
1 London Bridge Street
London SE1 9GF

www.harpercollins.co.uk

HarperCollins*Publishers*
Macken House, 39/40 Mayor Street Upper
Dublin 1, D01 C9W8, Ireland

First published by Thorsons 2024

10 9 8 7 6 5 4 3 2 1

Text © Tanya Mukendi 2024

Illustrations: Shutterstock.com

Tanya Mukendi asserts the moral right to be identified as the
author of this work

A catalogue record of this book is available from the British Library

ISBN 978-0-00-869526-2

Printed and bound in the UK using 100% renewable electricity at
CPI Group (UK) Ltd

This book is produced from independently certified FSC™ paper
to ensure responsible forest management.

For more information visit: www.harpercollins.co.uk/green

To the most compassionate and loving woman I know,
my dear mum. Your unwavering support and encouragement
have been the driving force behind all my endeavours.
This book is a tribute to your endless love and belief in me.
Thank you for being my guiding light.

CONTENTS

A LETTER FROM **TANYA**

Hello, my lovelies, I'm Tanya, your new BFF (Best Friend Forever) and home and cleaning enthusiast; thank you for choosing to buy my book. Or maybe you didn't, and you were gifted this rather than that iPad you wanted. Congrats, hun, you got me instead! Stick around, as I try to make it up to you with some witty banter and practical cleaning tips. So, make yourself a cuppa, get cosy and let's get into it.

Do you ever find yourself scrolling through your social-media feed wishing your home was as clean and organised as the ones you see on there? Have you thought that it's too expensive to buy all the various cleaning products and that you simply don't have enough space to store everything? Do you struggle with keeping your home tidy? If any of this sounds familiar, this book is perfect for you! Whether you're a beginner or an experienced cleaner seeking some motivation and fresh ideas, I have written a book packed full of tips and tricks to create a beautiful, organised home that you will love spending time in. This book offers hacks to organise your home without breaking the bank, and ways to increase your storage, as well as easy cleaning hacks that use common household items. My aim is to show you how to make your home beautiful and tidy in the shortest time possible, so you can focus on other things and live your best life.

Additionally, it provides ideas to reduce energy bills and help the environment through simple changes. With the cost of living constantly rising, this guidebook is a great resource for anyone looking to save some cash while maintaining a beautiful and functional home.

This book is your go-to guide for keeping your home beautiful, clean and organised. You can keep it on your bookshelf or leave it on your coffee table for quick access. Whether you've accidentally spilt red wine on your carpet, or you've just moved out of your family home for the first time and need help organising your new place, this book has got you covered!

My Story

If this is the first you've heard of me, let me introduce myself: I'm Tanya Mukendi of @tanyahomeinspo. I am a home hacks and cleaning content creator based in London. My passion is to help people with simple and quick home hacks that create time for other activities they enjoy. I first began posting home-improvement hacks in the middle of the Covid-19 pandemic. I was a key worker for the NHS at the time and so was in the midst of the chaos and working tirelessly to help others. I have always wanted a job in which I can make a difference and help others – I think it's just my nature.

I have always been a bit of a clean freak for as long as I can remember. I'm that annoying person chasing after my guests to put down coasters and wipe tables. I was definitely the Monica in my group of friends growing up. They have even noted that I sometimes greet them at the front door with a mop in my hand, and that my home always has that fresh, clean scent. This probably makes sense because mopping is always the last step in my cleaning routine. I love pouring a capful of my favourite floor cleaner into my bucket and mopping the floors with it. It's a real ritual for me.

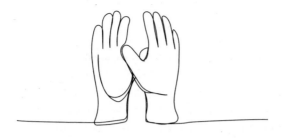

As I started working for the NHS and took on more roles and responsibilities, managing my home became challenging. My work demanded long hours, early starts and late finishes, and my time-management skills were poor. I lacked motivation, and the standards of my home were slipping more and more each day. Meanwhile, work was becoming increasingly hectic because of the pandemic. My modest one-bedroom flat never felt quite homely, cosy or organised, and I couldn't put my finger on why. Being busy with work and visiting loved ones was the distraction I needed to keep me away from home, as I rarely enjoyed being there anyway. However, the Covid lockdown forced me to be at home more often and face the reality of my living space.

Life was getting pretty chaotic for me, and I found myself desperately craving a little peace and quiet. And what better place to find it than at home, right? But there was just one problem – my home wasn't quite the oasis I wanted it to be. So I came up with a plan. Okay, okay, it was more like a little checklist scribbled on a piece of paper, but, hey, it was a start. I began by giving my house a really deep clean, and then I went on a bit of a shopping spree for some affordable decorations. I'll admit, I'm no professional decorator, so it was all a bit hit and miss. But I kept at it, cleaning, organising and decorating until my heart was content. And you know what? It turned out pretty darn great! My home has become my happy place, and I'm completely in love with it. By getting into a routine, finding ways to get motivated and making small changes, I was able to transform my living space, and it was all done on a budget. This is why I wanted to write this book. I want to put all the tools, tips and tricks I've learnt along the way into a book to help others who are also struggling.

I find cleaning therapeutic; for me, it is the ultimate form of self-care. Sharing my cleaning tips on my social-media channels @tanyahomeinspo has been such a comfort. It's amazing to see how many people out there feel the same way and support each other through their struggles. I never imagined that my humble cleaning tips would grow into a community of millions, all sharing the same desire to take care of their homes. I used to be all about going out, but now I'm a fully-fledged homebody and I love it! Plus, I've learnt that you don't have to spend a ton of money to make your home look and feel amazing. Even the smallest room can be turned into a cosy and relaxing sanctuary.

I know what you might be thinking: *It's easy for you to say, Tanya. You already have the skills and experience, and you enjoy cleaning.* But let me tell you, my lovelies, my journey to becoming a cleaning enthusiast was not always smooth sailing. Let's rewind for a second! I grew up in a household with my parents and four siblings – two older brothers, Junior and Rudy, and one older and one younger sister, Bilo and Wilma. Doing chores was part and parcel of our upbringing, and I was taught to do them from a very young age. I can't remember a time when we didn't have tasks around the house. Although my mum was very set in her ways and wanted everything to be neat and tidy, she also wanted us to learn life skills. I'll be honest – I didn't enjoy doing chores growing up, and I had to learn how to do them just like anyone else.

So here's a funny story about me and my older sister Bilo. I once wore her jacket without asking her permission, and while wearing it I accidentally spilt sauce on it. To fix the issue, I decided to wash it and put it back before she could notice. However, I didn't know that I wasn't supposed to tumble-dry it, and I ended up burning the jacket. My sister was very upset with me, but we eventually laughed it off. I learnt a valuable lesson that day: blame it on my younger sister next time! Just kidding, lol! I learnt that it is crucial to read and follow the washing instructions on labels. From that day onwards, I always make sure to read the labels before washing any clothes to avoid any more mishaps. It's important to take care of our clothes and look after those pennies, right?

Mum used to drive us crazy by constantly cleaning, organising and redecorating the house with items she found at charity shops or on the street. She was upcycling furniture before it became popular and taught me how to decorate my home affordably; I am definitely my mother's child. Although I initially disliked cleaning, I soon realised that it's a crucial part of maintaining a healthy and happy home. Eventually, I came to love and take pride in it. Growing up, my family instilled in me the importance of maintaining cleanliness and self-sufficiency. I attribute much of my inspiration and life lessons to my mother, who was an excellent role model in these areas.

So why have I chosen to focus on 'hacks', you might wonder? I absolutely love a life hack. The fact that you can use a clever little trick to shortcut your way into completing a task blows my mind. A good hack can save you money – and earn you bonus points for doing it in the quickest way possible, saving you time and effort. I believe I am a great problem-solver. I enjoy puzzles, quizzes, riddles – anything that requires critical thinking. It's the same with home hacks; whether it's removing a stain or finding a new decorating tip, I'm always on the lookout for ways to make my hacks accessible to all.

This is why I have written this book; I want to show you that cleaning can be enjoyable and, with the right tools and resources, doesn't have to be overwhelming. There are tips in here that will make keeping your home tidy much easier. Whether you have a laundry stain that you can't get out or a clogged sink, or you need some tips to help you stay motivated, I am here to help. I will show you how to look at your home with fresh eyes and help you recreate the space you want in a way that really works for you.

In this book, I cover all things home, including cleaning tips, home hacks, styling and organising. Most of the tips will be centred around budget-friendly and sustainable hacks, such as recipes for homemade cleaning products or tips on how to clean using products you already have around the house. This way, you can keep your house sparkling clean for a fraction of the price you might normally spend. We're all being more frugal right now, but that doesn't mean we have to compromise on our living space, and every little helps. Whether you're looking to save money on home decor, learn how to organise your home office or pack for a holiday - or perhaps learn how to create more storage in a house that feels smaller and smaller as your family grows – I've got you covered. If you're going to transform your home into the oasis it deserves to be, you're gonna need to take action. What you need is a friend to hold your hand along the way, a bestie to have your back and push you in the right direction. I volunteer.

Getting started can feel overwhelming, so I am here to guide you with some tips that you will be able to action straight away. Even if you hate cleaning, find it a chore or don't know how to motivate yourself to begin, I can find a way to help. We've all been there, when the only thing you want to do after getting home from a long day is put your feet up. However, trust me when I say that the rewards from actioning even the tiniest of changes in your home are priceless, and the costs are next to none. I always say, the best way to invest your time is in bettering yourself and your environment, and I couldn't be more passionate about spreading this message. Ultimately, I believe everyone's home should be their haven, their oasis. There's no place like home and I want to help you fall in love with yours.

Lots of love,

Tanya

PART 1

CLEANING HACKS

Whether you are a homeowner, renting your space, living alone or with your family, one of the most important things you can do is keep your home clean. Keeping your space in good condition helps to maintain your home's value, keeps it looking neat and tidy, and gives you a sense of accomplishment. By cleaning regularly, you can reduce stress, improve your mental health and boost productivity. Nothing beats the feeling of cosying up on the sofa, lighting a candle and relaxing in a beautiful home. Maintaining a clean home is the ultimate form of self-care. It not only brings you comfort, but also reduces the likelihood of health risks, as it gets rid of potential allergens by keeping dust and bacteria under control, and improves the overall indoor air quality. Also, if you have children or pets in the home, a cluttered space can create hazards. So, a cleaner home is a safer home.

I truly believe that everyone should treat themselves to a beautifully tidy and well-kept home. Don't worry if you have minimal cleaning skills; in this section, we will be covering the basics to get you that much closer to a cleaner and more organised home. My goal is to make this as simple as possible for you. So, let's get started!

Dos and Don'ts

It's really important to ensure we adopt and practise accurate and safe cleaning techniques. Why? To greatly reduce the risk of cross-contamination, and to avoid damaging your health and spreading germs and bacteria. So, let's run over some general cleaning dos and don'ts:

- Wear suitable protective gear, such as gloves, while cleaning.

- Always clean from the highest areas to the lowest.

- Clean from the back or the furthest point from the door to the front of the room.

- Do follow the manufacturer's instructions when handling chemicals.

- Do not store liquid products for longer than the manufacturer's instructions.

- Do not mix chemicals with other chemicals.

- Dry sweeping, mopping and dusting should be done carefully, to prevent dust, debris and microorganisms from getting into the air and landing on clean surfaces.

Store cleaning products safely and well out of reach of children and pets.

Cleaning with Common Household Items

Did you know that there are a few household items containing active ingredients that work as gentle cleansing agents? This means that you can use a few bits in your cupboard to clean around the home. It is always good to know that there are versatile products that can serve multiple purposes. Here's a list below, which I will be referencing throughout the book:

Item	Ways it can be used to clean
Shaving foam	Use to clean make-up stains, rugs/carpets, toilet bowls; neutralise urine smells; de-mist mirrors; polish chrome and stainless steel; clean jewellery.
Vinegar	Use to clean glass, countertops, taps, dishwashers, showers and bathtubs, appliances, toilets, floors.
Washing-up liquid (dish soap)	Use to mop floors; tackle oil stains; clean countertops, cooktops, refrigerators, microwaves, kitchen cabinets, barbeque grills, patio furniture, concrete slabs, windowsills.
Denture tablets	Use to sanitise toothbrushes; brighten dingy whites; clean toilet bowls, stained mugs, narrow vases, stained Tupperware, retainers and mouth guards, grout.
Dishwasher tablets	Use to clean washing machines, sinks, oven doors, air fryers, burnt pots and pans, oven racks, rubbish bins, litter boxes.

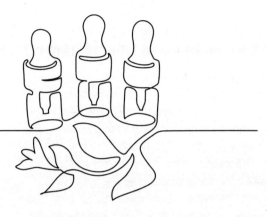

Using Essential Oils When You Have Pets

Essential oils are concentrated organic compounds produced by plants. People use essential oils for various purposes, including cleaning products, alternative medicines, flavourings, herbal remedies, personal care products, fragrances and more. As they are derived from plants, they are generally natural and safer than many commercial cleaning products containing chemicals. However, they can pose risks when used around our pets, so it's crucial to use them safely.

Some of the most common oils that are toxic to pets such as cats, dogs, birds, rabbits and guinea pigs include tea tree oil, cinnamon oil, eucalyptus oil, peppermint oil, clove oil, ylang-ylang oil and pine oil. These oils can cause a range of symptoms, including vomiting, diarrhoea and difficulty breathing. On the other hand, some essential oils are safe to use around cats and dogs, such as lavender, lemongrass, cedarwood, chamomile, frankincense, myrrh, ginger, rosemary and bergamot. Oils that are safe for birds, rabbits and guinea pigs are chamomile, clary sage, frankincense, ginger, cedarwood and myrrh. It's always a good idea to consult with a veterinarian before using any essential oils around your pets to be safe. If you're unsure whether an oil is safe or toxic for your pet, it's best to err on the side of caution and avoid using it altogether.

HOW TO USE ESSENTIAL OILS SAFELY AROUND YOUR PETS

If you're a pet owner who is fond of using essential oils around the house, it's important to take certain precautions to ensure the safety of your furry companions. One of the best ways to do this is by diluting the essential oils first and applying them to surfaces. Do not use them directly on your pets. Also, make sure that all essential oils are kept out of your pet's reach, regardless of whether or not they are considered toxic. If you're using essential oils for cleaning, it's best to do so when your pet is not around and to let the surfaces dry completely before allowing your pet to come into contact with them. Additionally, be mindful that some essential-oil products may contain other substances, so it's always best to opt for 100 per cent natural essential oils.

Mental Health and Cleaning

Many of us have experienced the therapeutic effects of cleaning. The act of decluttering and tidying up can help clear our minds and reduce stress. In fact, research shows that a clean and organised living space can have a positive impact on our mental health. When we are surrounded by clutter and mess, it can be challenging to focus on anything else. This can lead to feelings of anxiety, overwhelm and even depression. On the other hand, a clean and organised environment can help create a sense of calm and order, which can have a positive impact on our mental well-being.

Moreover, cleaning can also serve as a form of exercise, which is known to have mental-health benefits. Physical activity has been shown to reduce stress, anxiety and depression, and cleaning can provide an opportunity to move our bodies and release endorphins.

However, it's important to note that cleaning should not be used as a coping mechanism for mental-health issues. A clean and organised living space can help improve our mental well-being, by reducing stress and anxiety, but it's important to approach cleaning as a tool for self-care, rather than a way to avoid dealing with deeper issues. Cleaning cannot replace therapy or medication, and it's essential to seek professional help if you're struggling with mental-health issues. By prioritising our mental health, we can then use cleaning to achieve a healthy living space that supports our overall well-being.

Some of you who have been following me for a while may already know that my dad passed away a few years ago. I know first-hand what it feels like when life knocks you down. During that period, I was just in the midst of going viral on social media, and a few of my hacks were featured in national and international news articles. What should have been an exciting time for me turned out to be one of the hardest times of my life. However, I found that cleaning and organising helped me through the tough times. It helped me take my mind off it. Sometimes I wonder about my dad, and I wish he was here to see it all – he would have been so proud. I must say his passing is what drove me to fulfil my dream.

There's no rulebook on how to deal with grief; there's no right or wrong way. Each and every one of my four siblings, all going through the same experience, dealt with it differently. With me, it triggered my anxiety. I had days when I didn't want to do anything, and some days I would get up and clean obsessively. It was the only thing I could do to distract myself.

Unfortunately, there will be times in your life when things happen that you can't control. My advice to you is to be patient with yourself. In time, things will be okay again. In these times, it's important to take care of yourself and prioritise your mental health. Whether you're dealing with grief or any other traumatic experience in your life, rely on your support system. Don't be afraid to ask for help; people are there and want to offer support. That's what life is about: helping others in times of need.

CHAPTER 1

MAKING A START

Have you ever looked at a sink full of dirty dishes or a cluttered bedroom and thought to yourself, *Didn't I just clean this?* Sometimes it can feel like you're in a never-ending cycle of cleaning. It can be extremely daunting to look at a messy and disorganised home and imagine getting started. One look at the mess and you're ready to throw the towel in before you've even begun. You are not alone, trust me. Decision fatigue is real, and it can lead you to procrastinate or give up altogether. Feeling overwhelmed is completely normal, but it's important to know that with a little bit of willpower and structure, you can completely transform your living space.

I would start by taking a look around and writing down the areas you want to tackle. Are there cupboards that need to be decluttered? Are there piles of clothes that need washing? Do you need to give your toilet a deep clean? Whether you need to cleanse your entire house or just do a general spot tidy, noting things down is the first step to getting organised. If I am feeling anxious about a particular task, writing it down helps to clear my mind. Once you write everything down, you'll notice an instant sense of relief, as if a weight has been lifted off you. Remember that any small bit of progress is an accomplishment and will motivate you to continue. Take a deep breath and take the first step.

Still not sure how to take the first step? Here are some good places to get started:

- **The floor:** Tackling the floor first can go a long way in improving the overall appearance of a room. Start by sorting through piles of mail or arranging books, sweeping up crumbs or vacuuming the living-room rug. A cluttered or dirty floor can make everything else in the room appear messier than it is, so starting here can make a big impact.

- **The kitchen sink:** If there are any dishes in the sink, wash them or load them into the dishwasher. After that, it's a good idea to scrub the sink itself. To protect your sink from water stains, you can dry the sink after rinsing it. By doing this, you'll have a clean and shiny sink in no time, which will give you a great sense of accomplishment and motivation to move on to the next task.

- **The laundry basket:** The laundry basket is a great task to tackle first, as while your dirty clothes take a spin in the suds, you'll be able to use that time to tackle other tasks.

- **The toilet:** This might often feel like the last thing you want to do, but it's an important one and, if done correctly, the toilet can be cleaned in only five minutes. Spray toilet cleaner all over the toilet and wipe it all away with kitchen roll, or you could use antibacterial cleaning wipes. Be sure to work from top to bottom, and don't forget to scrub the toilet bowl with a scrubbing brush and toilet-bowl cleaner. You'll feel accomplishment in a matter of minutes, then you can move on to the next task.

Figure Out Your Priorities

If you tend to get stressed out by house cleaning, it's helpful to take a proactive approach. Make a list of the specific cleaning tasks that give you the greatest sense of accomplishment or have the biggest impact on your home. You don't have to include every possible cleaning project, room or surface – just focus on what matters most to you. Use a note-taking app on your phone or write it out on paper and stick it to the fridge for easy reference. When you're feeling overwhelmed, refer to your list and start with a task that you haven't completed yet.

Here are some scenarios to help you determine your cleaning priorities. Imagine you had guests coming over this weekend. What cleaning tasks would be an absolute non-negotiable no-fail before they arrived? If you work from home, what chores need to be completed in order for you to concentrate properly? Or even when you're relaxing and enjoying free time, either with your family or by yourself? Are there any specific messes that would keep you from being able to relax and have fun?

Ask yourself these questions and use the answers as a basis to start figuring out your priorities and where to start.

Train Your Brain for Motivation

It can be extremely difficult to find the motivation to work on your home when you are already feeling overwhelmed. I'd love to tell you that I've always been the girl with a perfectly clean home, but we're friends, and friends don't lie to each other. I've had my fair share of overflowing laundry, dishes piled in the sink and dust up to my eyeballs. And there have been several instances when I had zero motivation to clean. If this sounds like you, I want you to take a deep breath. Help is available – you are not alone, and you can regain control of your home.

The truth is that everyone enjoys having a clean house, but not everyone enjoys cleaning. It's okay to feel unmotivated to clean; trust me, I get it. Working long hours, running around after the little ones, feeling run down or not feeling up to it – sometimes life just gets in the way. That does not make you lazy; it makes you (drumroll, please ...) human. If you're anything like me, you will find a hundred reasons to procrastinate. Luckily, there are many ways you can get motivated to clean your home even when you're not up to it.

TAKE BEFORE AND AFTER PICTURES

How satisfying are the before and afters? I've always enjoyed them. Turns out, they aren't just for your fitness goals. I find that taking some before and after pictures or videos of a messy house can be a fantastic way to track your progress and give you a visual representation of how much you've accomplished, all of which has the effect of keeping you motivated and on track to complete your goals.

MAKE YOUR OWN OR BUY SOME NEW CLEANING PRODUCTS

I've noticed that buying or making a new cleaning product can really get me in the mood to tidy up. It's like buying new gym clothes to motivate you to exercise. It's exciting to try out new products and see how effective they are, and the fresh scent always adds a little extra motivation. Plus, using your favourite cleaning tools can make the whole experience even more enjoyable. So, if you're feeling a little sluggish in the cleaning department, maybe treat yourself to some new supplies, or see page 27 for some recipes to make your own, and see if that helps get you going!

REMOVE DISTRACTIONS

Let's be real, cleaning can be a daunting task, especially when you're feeling unenthused. It can be tough enough as it is to get motivated to clean, and the last thing you need are added distractions pulling you away from your tasks. One way to stay focused is to put your phone away so you're not tempted to check it every time you get a notification. It's also best to avoid catching up on gossip with your bestie or watching your favourite Netflix series while cleaning, as these distractions will only slow you down. Trust me, the fewer visual distractions you have, the faster you'll be able to get your tasks done and get back to doing other things.

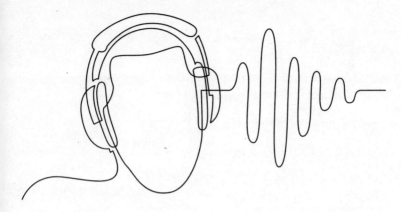

TURN UP THE SOUND

This is one that can really help you get in the zone! I don't know about you, but cleaning while listening to Nineties R'n'B is on another level. I've definitely twerked in the kitchen with my Marigolds on while listening to Beyoncé's 'Single Ladies' one too many times. I've mopped to Ed Sheeran, dusted while rapping to Nicki Minaj and ironed while singing along to Whitney.

I've found that having some background music while cleaning can really make the whole experience more enjoyable. Not only does it help keep me motivated, but it can also turn cleaning into a fun activity rather than a dreaded chore. I mean, who doesn't feel inspired while listening to their favourite tunes? So, no matter what kind of music you're into, I highly recommend giving it a try and seeing if it makes your cleaning routine a whole lot more satisfying!

LISTEN TO PODCASTS

Podcasts are another great source of entertainment while cleaning; keeping you engaged and focused during mundane tasks like folding laundry or scrubbing dishes. You could listen to a podcast episode or turn on an audiobook, or anything that catches your attention and helps you relax while getting your cleaning done. It's a great way to make the task less stressful and more enjoyable.

SET A TIMER

If you're finding it hard to get motivated, don't worry! I have another trick up my sleeve that works well for me. Try this:

- Set a timer for 30 minutes.

- Use those 30 minutes to clean.

- Take a 10-minute break from cleaning.

- Then repeat if needed.

If 30 minutes doesn't work for you then adjust the timing to suit your needs. Don't feel like you have to clean for hours on end. Start with just five minutes of cleaning if you prefer – remember that starting small is still starting, so begin with achievable goals. Don't worry about sticking to a strict schedule. The idea is to train your brain to associate cleaning with short, relaxed bursts of activity. This will help you make steady progress towards a cleaner and more organised home without feeling overwhelmed. And who knows? Maybe tidying up your home will be more fun if you give yourself a hard deadline to beat!

WATCH CLEANING-MOTIVATION VIDEOS

If you're still struggling to find the motivation to clean your home, you might want to consider watching cleaning-motivation videos. These videos, made by creators on social-media platforms such as YouTube, TikTok and Instagram, are designed to inspire you to clean your home. While it may seem counterintuitive to watch others clean to get motivated, there is something satisfying about watching someone transform their messy home into a clean one. These videos have helped me a lot when I've been feeling uninspired and low on energy, and I think they could help you too. If you're interested, feel free to check out my page @tanyahomeinspo for some cleaning-motivation videos. Just be careful not to get sucked into the TikTok rabbit hole, and remember to watch only a couple before getting to work.

PREPARE YOUR CLEANING KIT

Putting together your cleaning kit can be a really fun way to prepare for a cleaning session and get in the right headspace. For me, having everything I need in one place really gets me in the mood to clean. It's like giving a child sugar – you get an instant burst of energy!

Here's the thing: there's no right or wrong way to put together a cleaning kit. What you put in your cleaning caddy is totes up to you, babe! You know your home better than anyone, so you can choose the cleaning essentials that work for you and your home. If you're only planning on mopping your floors, then you don't need to grab every cleaning product in your cupboard. In most cases, I simply grab a multi-purpose spray and a cloth and I'm good to go. However, when I'm planning to clean multiple rooms at home, I tend to put together a simple cleaning kit. Cleaning is more fun when you have supplies that are coordinated and work well. Gathering the supplies in advance will also save you time and energy.

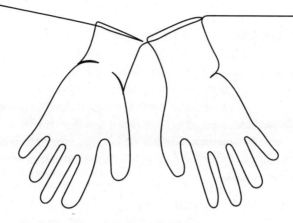

Here is an example of a useful cleaning kit:

Simple cleaning kit

- Multi-purpose cleaner

- Glass and mirror cleaner

- Toilet cleaner

- Disinfectant or antibacterial wipes

- Microfibre cloths

- Duster

- Scrubbing brush

- Sponges

- Rubber gloves

- Bin bags

- Kitchen towel

Remember, what you put in your cleaning kit is entirely up to you. Don't overthink it, and choose the cleaning supplies that work best for you and your home.

Natural Cleaning Products

As my wise Congolese mother always says, 'You don't need all those fancy cleaning products to keep your home clean. Just use what you already have in the cupboard.' Of course, she doesn't mean you should grab the milk from the fridge and start cleaning your toilet with it, but there are definitely things you can find at home that will do the job just as well as a branded cleaner.

Since becoming a cleaning content creator, I've made a few lifestyle changes. Gone are the days of buying every single cleaning product out there (trust me, that was a hard habit to quit). I have learnt so much about how to clean your house effectively and in the safest ways possible. I have really embraced using natural cleaning products, and I love experimenting and coming up with my own recipes. Don't get me wrong, this doesn't mean I won't ever use shop-bought cleaning products. There are some shop-bought cleaning staples that I love, that work well and that I have been using for years. It's not about cutting shop-bought cleaning products out altogether, it's about balance and being mindful of what we are using to clean our homes. In the current climate, we are all on a budget and can't afford to splurge on every latest cleaning product out there - not to mention the health and environmental advantages of homemade products too.

Making your own natural cleaning products offers a number of benefits. By using natural ingredients like baking soda, white vinegar and lemon, you can avoid exposure to the harmful chemicals found in many commercial cleaning products. Additionally, you can customise your cleaning solutions to suit your specific cleaning needs and preferences. And last but not least, creating your own cleaning products is a fun and rewarding DIY activity that can save you money in the long run. Here are some natural cleaning products that you can make at home:

DIY NATURAL CLEANING PRODUCTS RECIPES

Supplies/ingredients: Baking soda, distilled white vinegar, washing-up liquid (dish soap), surgical spirit (rubbing alcohol) and hydrogen peroxide (see box below), olive oil, essential oils of your choice (eucalyptus and lavender are particularly good to use as they have disinfectant properties), 3 × 250ml spray bottles, 1 × 250ml bottle with cap, 1 × 100ml spice jar with sifter, 1 × 250ml opaque spray bottle (as hydrogen peroxide is sensitive to light). If you don't have a 250ml spray bottle to hand, don't worry. The recipes provided can be easily adjusted to fit the size of your bottle. Simply double or reduce the ingredients as needed.

Multi-purpose cleaner: 125ml (½ cup) white vinegar, 125ml (½ cup) water, 10 drops of essential oil, 3 drops of washing-up liquid (dish soap). Makes a 250ml-sized bottle.

Dusting spray: 160ml (¾ cup) water, 60ml (¼ cup) white vinegar, 10 drops of essential oil, 2 tablespoons of olive oil. Makes a 250ml-sized bottle.

Glass and mirror cleaner: 125ml (½ cup) white vinegar, 125ml (½ cup) water. Makes a 250ml-sized bottle.

Deodoriser: 100g (½ cup) baking soda, 10 drops of essential oil per 100ml spice jar.

Disinfectant spray: 125ml (½ cup) hydrogen peroxide, 125ml (½ cup) water, 10 drops of essential oil. Makes a 250ml-sized bottle (put into an opaque spray bottle).

Floor cleaner: 125ml (½ cup) water, 60ml (¼ cup) white vinegar, 60ml (¼ cup) rubbing alcohol (this ingredient is very low on the toxicity scale), 10 drops of essential oil, 3 drops of washing-up liquid (dish soap). Makes a 250ml-sized bottle.

A NOTE ON RUBBING ALCOHOL AND HYDROGEN PEROXIDE

Rubbing alcohol/surgical spirit and hydrogen peroxide are disinfectants commonly used to sanitise surfaces in households. Rubbing alcohol is a solution of isopropyl alcohol in water that typically consists of 70 per cent alcohol. Hydrogen peroxide is a chemical compound containing hydrogen and oxygen in clear liquid form. These disinfectants are readily available at most pharmacies, online marketplaces such as Amazon and supermarkets, and can usually be found in the first-aid or cleaning-supplies section. To ensure safety, it is recommended that you wear gloves while handling them to avoid contact with your skin. Also, it is essential to store them in secure and safe locations, out of reach of children and pets, as they can be hazardous if misused or ingested. In case you prefer natural alternatives, you can use lemon juice or vinegar instead of chemicals.

CHAPTER 2

KITCHEN HACKS

My mum, Aimé (which means 'love' in French), always says, 'The kitchen is the heart of the home.' She says, 'It's where we spend a lot of our time making food we love for the people we love.' She is a wise woman and I love her to bits, but I wish she had warned me that I would be cleaning my kitchen every day for the rest of my life! There's nothing more satisfying than a clean kitchen, but gosh, the cleaning can seem never-ending, can't it? You spend hours cleaning it, and before you know it, it's messy again, especially with us all spending more time at home than we ever have before.

I don't know about you, but when my kitchen is messy, I'm way more likely to order food in and skip cooking altogether. A clean and organised kitchen without spills and dirty dishes piled up in the sink is so much more inviting!

There are simple tips and tricks you can follow to make the process of cleaning your kitchen easier. For example, try to clean up spills and messes as soon as they happen to prevent them from becoming more significant problems later on. You can also do small cleaning tasks throughout the day, like wiping down counters or washing dishes, to prevent an enormous build-up of mess. And remember, a little bit of organisation can go a long way in making your kitchen feel cleaner and more manageable.

So, first, let's delve into some of my top tips so that you can work out how to clean your kitchen with ease, and cut down on the time you spend doing it.

Cleaning Your Sink

If you're anything like me, your kitchen is probably the first room to get messy and cluttered. You can work hard at keeping it tidy, but there always seems to be another cleaning task to be done, especially if you love cooking or enjoy getting creative with messy DIY projects. So, it's no surprise that your sink might get dirty really quickly.

CLEAN THE SINK USING LEMON AND BAKING SODA

An effective way to clean your sink is by using baking soda and lemon. First, sprinkle baking soda liberally over the entire surface of your sink. Then, slice a lemon in half and squeeze one half over the baking soda. Using the other half of the lemon, rub it over the baking soda in a circular motion. This will help to deodorise the sink while the baking soda polishes the surface. Finally, rinse off and enjoy the shine.

It's worth noting that you may have different types of sinks in your home, such as stainless steel, porcelain, ceramic, granite, composite or copper. However, as lemon is a natural cleaner, you can use this hack to clean all types of sink materials.

FRESHEN AND UNCLOG THE SINK USING LEMON

Not only will lemon and baking soda leave your sink sparkling clean, but it will help unclog your drains too. Food scraps, soap scum, dead skin cells and human or pet hair are just some of the things you regularly wash down your sink, shower or bath plughole. So it's no wonder you may experience a clogged drain from time to time, but don't fret! There is an easy solution you can try before calling a plumber.

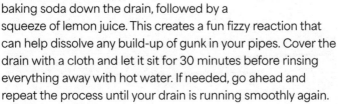

First, run hot water in the affected sink or shower for a few minutes. Then, slowly pour 100g (½ cup) of baking soda down the drain, followed by a squeeze of lemon juice. This creates a fun fizzy reaction that can help dissolve any build-up of gunk in your pipes. Cover the drain with a cloth and let it sit for 30 minutes before rinsing everything away with hot water. If needed, go ahead and repeat the process until your drain is running smoothly again.

MAKE YOUR STAINLESS STEEL SPARKLE

Stainless steel is extremely popular in kitchens and bathrooms, but it can be a bother to preserve, as it's prone to showing marks and can often look quite dull.

It's fine to clean your stainless-steel appliances with an all-purpose cleaner, or maybe even just a dampened microfibre cloth. But to make it shine, you'll need to polish it. A touch of baby oil, coconut oil or olive oil buffed into the surface with a soft cloth or paper towel is all you need to make it gleam.

USE A BAG OF VINEGAR TO IMPROVE TAP FLOW

Did you know that hard water can make your taps look unsightly and even lead to slow water flow in some areas of your home? But fear not, there's a simple and cost-effective solution to this problem! All you need to do is fill a sandwich bag with vinegar, tie it around your kitchen taps with an elastic band to seal it and leave it overnight. The vinegar will work to clean the hard water build-up on both the interior and exterior surfaces of the tap, making them look as good as new and improving water flow. You can use this hack for other taps in your home too, such as those in your bathroom or utility sink. You can also use it to clean your shower head. There's no need for expensive household cleaners when you can easily tackle this problem with vinegar!

Cleaning Your Oven

Of all the household chores that we dread, cleaning the oven has got to be near the top of the list. It's time-consuming, uncomfortable and often a gross task, especially if it has been put off for a while. But I have some hacks to help you face this daunting task.

USE A DISHWASHER TABLET TO CLEAN GREASY OVEN DOORS

A simple dishwashing tablet can easily remove stubborn, baked-on grease from your oven door? It's true! Trust me, if you ignore cleaning your oven door, it'll become a nightmare to clean later on. But with this hack, you can clean away the grease with ease and no mess. Simply put on some gloves, dip the dishwashing tablet in warm water and scrub the oven door using the tablet. Keep dipping the tablet back into the water to keep it moist and rub it all over the oven door until the grease has vanished. It's that easy! Just make sure to use the hard type of dishwashing tablet, not the gel pods, for best results.

USE A HOMEMADE RECIPE TO CLEAN INSIDE YOUR OVEN

Cleaning the inside of your oven regularly is important for many reasons. First, it helps to remove built-up grease and food debris that can become a fire hazard. Also, a dirty oven

HOW TO MAKE OVEN CLEANER

Ingredients:
120g (½ cup) baking soda
125ml (½ cup) warm water
1 tablespoon of washing-up liquid (dish soap)

Method: To clean your oven, start by mixing the baking soda, water and washing-up liquid (dish soap) until you have a paste. Take out the oven racks and trays, and then use a sponge or a soft-bristled brush to apply the paste to the oven. Leave the oven door open to prevent any build-up of fumes inside. Let the paste sit for 20 minutes, then scrub away until the oven is clean. You can also use a plastic scraper to help remove any tough stains. For the racks and trays, apply the paste and let it sit for 20 minutes before scrubbing them clean.

can affect the taste and quality of your food. Finally, a clean oven will help it work more efficiently, which can save you money on energy bills in the long run. See above for a great recipe for homemade oven cleaner.

COOK LEMON IN THE OVEN TO MELT AWAY GREASE

To freshen up your oven and melt away any grease, follow these simple steps. First, cut a lemon into slices and place them in a roasting tin filled with water. Then, heat up the tin in the oven at a low temperature (between 120°C/250°F and 150°C/300°F) for 30 minutes. Once the time is up, let the roasting tin cool until it's lukewarm before dipping a cloth into the lemon water. Use the cloth to wipe down your oven - the steam will melt away the grease, making it easier to wipe away, and the lemon will give your oven a fresh scent.

CLEANING OVEN HOBS/STOVETOPS

Cleaning your oven hob doesn't have to be a difficult task; with the right approach, it can be done easily and effectively. Here are some tips for cleaning different types of hobs:

- **For induction hobs**, use a soft cloth or sponge and a mild detergent to clean the surface. Avoid using abrasive or harsh cleaning agents that can scratch or damage the surface. For stubborn stains, you can use a special cleaner designed for induction hobs.

- **For gas hobs**, remove the grates and burners and soak them in hot soapy water for at least 30 minutes. Use a soft brush or toothbrush to scrub away any stubborn stains or debris. For the hob itself, use a soft cloth or sponge and a mild detergent to clean the surface. Avoid using abrasive or harsh cleaning agents that can scratch or damage the surface.

- **For ceramic hobs**, use a soft cloth or sponge and a ceramic hob cleaner to clean the surface. Avoid using abrasive or harsh cleaning agents that can scratch or damage the surface. For stubborn stains, you can use a razor blade to gently scrape away the debris. Be sure to use a gentle touch and avoid applying too much pressure, as this can damage the surface.

Regardless of the type of oven hob, it's important to clean it regularly to prevent build-up of grease and grime. By following these tips, you can keep your oven hobs looking clean and new for longer.

Burnt-on grease on hobs/stovetops

One of the most common questions I get asked is how to remove burnt-on grease on oven hobs. It doesn't matter whether you have a ceramic, gas or induction hob; food can burn and get stuck, making it a pain to clean. We all know the best way to prevent spills and splatters from hardening is to clean the stove immediately after cooking. However, more often than not, this remains wishful thinking, and we postpone the job for another day. So, what to do when you have stubborn, burnt-on grease? Well, you could always try chanting some cleaning mantras or pleading with the grease to come off, but I'm not sure that'll do the trick.

Instead, use a thick cream cleaner (Cif is my favourite) or make a paste of baking soda and washing-up liquid (dish soap). Apply the cleaner to your hob with gloves on and use a non-scratch hob scraper to remove the grease. This tool is perfect for ceramic and glass hobs. The paste will help break down the tough stains and make it easier to clean your hob. Just make sure to rinse off the paste thoroughly with warm water and dry with a clean cloth. This method is much more effective and less time-consuming than scrubbing with a scourer, and your hob will look as good as new.

CLEAN OVEN RACKS WITHOUT SCRUBBING

Cleaning oven racks can be a daunting task, and it's not uncommon to struggle with it. I remember going through some tough times trying to get my oven racks clean. It was probably one of the messiest cleans I did. I used to scrub the shelves vigorously with a scourer and ended up splashing brown grease all over my clothes, the sink and the floors. At times, I even got it in my eye, which was quite painful. It didn't help that my sink wasn't big enough to fit the racks in, so I had to clean them at an awkward angle. My hands would ache from all that scrubbing, and it was honestly a nightmare. However, I eventually learnt a simple and easy way to clean my oven racks, and I'm so glad I did.

Lay an old towel in the bottom of your bathtub, place the oven racks on top of it and then fill the tub with warm water. Dissolve one (or two if the rack is caked with a lot of grease) dishwasher tablet in the bath and leave the oven racks to soak overnight. In the morning, rinse them off and wipe away any remaining grime with a sponge. This simple hack will make cleaning your oven racks a breeze and save you from the tedious task of scrubbing them by hand. Make sure you rinse your bath well with hot water afterwards before using it again.

STEAM-CLEAN YOUR DIRTY MICROWAVE

Oh, the dreaded *POP!* of food being splattered inside the microwave - there's nothing worse, is there? I have definitely exploded food in the microwave one too many times. Cleaning your microwave can be a pain, especially if there are stubborn food stains and odours to deal with. However, you can easily clean your microwave in less than 10 minutes without using harsh chemicals. All you need is a microwaveable bowl, water and vinegar. First, fill the bowl with 500ml (2 cups) of water and add 2 tablespoons of vinegar. Next, put the bowl in the microwave, shut the door and run the microwave on high for five minutes. When the timer goes off, leave the door shut for two to three more minutes to let the steam continue to work; it will help loosen up caked-on bits of food and eliminate any odours. Finally,

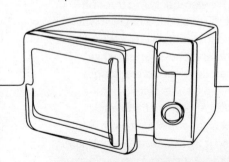

take your sponge and wipe down the inside of the microwave - the dirt and food will come right off!

TANYA'S TIP

Drop a toothpick into the bowl before putting it into the microwave to prevent the water from boiling up over the edges.

Cleaning Your Fridge

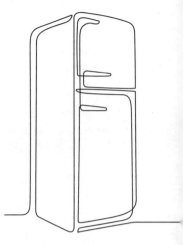

It can be quite off-putting to eat food from a smelly fridge, can't it? Opening up your fridge and having your nostrils hit with the smell of mouldy broccoli is hardly appetising. Keeping your fridge clean not only keeps it odourless, but actually keeps food fresher for longer, which means less mouldy food and less cleaning in the long run – win-win!

HOW TO DEEP CLEAN YOUR FRIDGE

To prevent any bacteria, mould growth and smelly outbreaks, it's essential to keep your fridge clean. I usually do a quick wipe down once a week, but every three months or so, I try to do a more thorough deep clean of my fridge.

1 The first step is to remove all the food, bottles and jars from the fridge. Also, take out all the compartments and shelves.

2 Throwing out any expired food is a good idea, especially if it's been buried and forgotten at the back of the fridge. There's no point in going to all the trouble of cleaning and organising the fridge, just to put back in smelly and spoilt food.

3 Next, turn off your refrigerator and wait until it returns to room temperature.

4 Now it's time to put on your favourite cleaning gloves, grab your trusty cleaning spray and get ready to make your fridge sparkle! Spray your fridge cleaner (see recipe below) on the outside and inside of the empty fridge. Leave the solution on the inside for five minutes, then wipe it down with a microfibre cloth moistened with warm water. This will help get rid of any food or spills and musty smells. For tough stains,

saturate a cloth in the cleaning solution and place it on the area for 15 minutes. Wipe away residue to remove.

5 Don't forget to clean the doors, and the top and bottom of the refrigerator. Additionally, use cotton swabs and toothpicks to clean the small areas that are tough to wipe clean, such as the seals around the door or the handles.

6 Scrub the compartments and shelves with soapy water and mist with a natural cleaning spray (see my all-natural fridge cleaner recipe below) to tackle stubborn grime.

7 Finally, dry your fridge and its compartments with a clean cloth, put everything back in place and switch the fridge back on. Easy-peasy.

TANYA'S TIP

Take a before photo of the fridge to remember where each compartment is located.

TANYA'S TIP

When cleaning up spills from raw meat or fish in your fridge, it's important to clean them up properly. Do this by wiping up the spill with a paper towel or cloth, then disinfect the area. If you're out of disinfectant solution, use a small amount of hydrogen peroxide or rubbing alcohol (see page 28), as they both kill a wide variety of germs (including bacteria, viruses and fungi). Let the solution sit for at least five minutes, then wipe it dry with a clean cloth. This will help to ensure that harmful bacteria are eliminated and that your fridge remains a safe place for storing food.

WHY YOU SHOULD USE AN ALL-NATURAL CLEANER IN THE FRIDGE

If you're like me, you want your fridge to be clean and smell fresh all the time, so it's tempting to grab the best-smelling kitchen cleaner you can find and spray it all over your fridge until it smells like lemons or strawberries or whatever your favourite scent is. That's a big no! I had to learn the hard way NEVER to do this. Once, I cleaned my fridge using a commercial cleaner, and my food tasted terrible because it was contaminated with chemicals. It was a miracle that I didn't get sick. By using commercial cleaners, you will be spraying all sorts of harmful chemicals into your fridge that can contaminate your food. Therefore, it is best to avoid using chemicals altogether.

Don't get me wrong, I'm pretty adventurous with foods. However, I definitely don't want the taste of cleaning products in my dinner! No way! That would not be a pleasant experience. Using ingredients like baking soda, vinegar and lemon juice is a much safer option. Making your own homemade natural cleaner is more effective and won't leave any harmful residue. Plus, it'll leave your fridge smelling fresh and clean! So, next time your fridge smells off, remember to opt for a natural solution instead of a commercial one - try using the recipe below.

HOW TO MAKE HOMEMADE FRIDGE SPRAY

Ingredients:
60ml (¼ cup) vinegar
170ml (¾ cup) warm water
1 tablespoon of vanilla extract

Method: Pour the vinegar, warm water and vanilla extract into a 250ml glass spray bottle, give it a good shake and it's ready to go. The best part? The spray is made from all-natural ingredients that you may already have in your cupboard.

NEUTRALISE FRIDGE ODOURS

At times, refrigerator odours can linger even after you clean them. I have to confess that I have left uncovered food in my fridge, causing some pretty funky odours. Onions, garlic and mouldy foods are just a few culprits that have made my fridge smell, even long after I have taken them out. But let's be real: onions and garlic shouldn't even be in the fridge in the first place, so I guess we can't blame the fridge entirely. Luckily, the funky smells are easily resolved, and you can get your fridge smelling great again.

To do this, try making this simple odour-absorbing mixture below using baking soda, salt and essential oil.

MAKE YOUR OWN ODOUR-ABSORBER

Ingredients:
120g (½ cup) baking soda
70g (¼ cup) salt
20 drops of essential oil

Method: First, mix the baking soda, salt and essential oil in a jar. Stir the mixture well and place the open jar at the back of the fridge (add a label to warn people that it is not food!). This will quickly absorb any unpleasant odours. Remember to replace the baking soda mixture every one to two months to keep your fridge smelling fresh and clean. If you don't want to use essential oils, you can simply put a box of baking soda in the fridge to help absorb odours and keep the fridge smelling fresh between deep cleans.

Cleaning Your Dishwasher

You know what's funny? I don't have a dishwasher, but I've always dreamt of having one. I mean, who doesn't love the idea of loading and unloading dishes without actually having to scrub them by hand? Unfortunately, my modest London flat doesn't have the space for such a luxury. But, hey, a girl can dream, right? Just remember the next time you're unloading your dishwasher, there's someone out there who's green with envy.

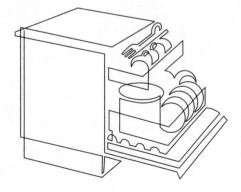

I may not have my own dishwasher, but I've got plenty of experience of cleaning them from my days working at a care home. It may not be the most exciting chore, but it's essential to keep it running well and prevent odours and grimy build-up. Purchasing dishwasher cleaning products can be expensive, but luckily, you can clean your dishwasher using a natural and cheaper alternative.

HOW TO CLEAN A DISHWASHER

Clean your dishwasher once a month to make it last longer. As the saying goes, 'Clean the things that clean.'

1 Remove any food debris or solid matter from the dishwasher's filter and spray arm.

2 Pour 250ml (1 cup) of white vinegar into a dishwasher-safe container and place it on the top rack of your dishwasher. Run the dishwasher on the hottest cycle possible.

3 Once the vinegar cycle is complete, sprinkle 120g (½ cup) of baking soda on the bottom of the dishwasher and run another hot cycle.

4 Use a damp cloth to wipe down the interior of the dishwasher, paying special attention to the corners and crevices where food and grime can build up.

5 Use a gentle cleaner or a mixture of warm water and vinegar to clean the exterior of the dishwasher, including the door, handle and control panel.

By following these simple steps, you can keep your dishwasher running smoothly and smelling fresh.

Cleaning Your Wooden Chopping Boards

I am just obsessed with my wooden chopping boards; they are eco-friendly and add a touch of elegance to your kitchen. You'd probably find one in every corner of my kitchen. They just look beautiful on your shelves and worktops. And not only are they a pleasure to chop on, but they also keep your knife blades sharper for longer. However, the downside is that they can require a bit more maintenance than plastic boards. Knowing how to clean a wooden chopping board properly is essential for keeping it germ-free, for general food safety and for making it last longer.

1 CLEAN THE BOARD

To clean a wooden chopping board, firstly scrape away any debris. Then, gently scrub the board with a sponge and hot, soapy water. It's important to wash both sides of the board, even if you only used one side, to prevent uneven drying that could cause the wood to warp. Rinse the board and dry it thoroughly with a clean tea towel or paper towel. To prevent any residual water from pooling on the surface, stand the board upright on your counter and let it air-dry completely before storing it.

TANYA'S TIP

Never put your wooden chopping board in the dishwasher or submerge it in a sink full of water as this can cause warping and cracking. Over time, little cuts and grooves may develop in the board, which can become a breeding ground for bacteria. This can lead to cross-contamination when using the board for different types of food such as poultry, fish and vegetables.

2 SANITISE AND DEODORISE

If your chopping board has picked up any strong smells from foods such as garlic and onions, you can easily remove the odour. To do this, sprinkle salt or baking soda over the surface of the board. Cut a lemon in half and use one half to scrub the board, squeezing out the juice as you go. The acid from the lemon will help disinfect the board and neutralise any odours. Rinse the board with hot water and dry it thoroughly with a clean towel.

3 TREAT THE BOARD

To prevent your chopping board from drying out and cracking over time, it's important to treat it with a food-safe mineral oil every few months. Some suggestions include Materialix Food Grade Mineral Oil, T&G Food Safe Wood Oil or Furniture Clinic Cutting Board Oil. You can buy these from home stores, DIY stores, supermarkets and online stores such as Amazon. This treatment will help keep the wood moisturised and in good condition for longer. Pour a few tablespoons of the oil onto the surface of the board, once it is clean and dry. Using a soft cloth or paper towel, gently rub in the oil in slow circular motions, ensuring that you cover all surfaces of the chopping board. After that, use clean cloths to wipe the board dry as best you can. Finally, let the board air-dry overnight. This process will help keep your wooden chopping board in good condition for a long time.

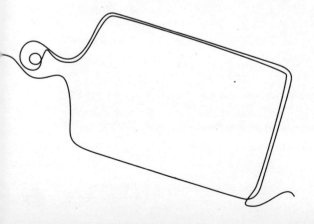

General Kitchen Tips

Last of all, here are a few more hacks for those regular kitchen-cleaning essentials.

HOW TO CLEAN THE TOASTER

Cleaning a toaster may seem like a daunting task, but it's actually quite simple. First and foremost, make sure to unplug the toaster and let it cool down completely. Then, remove the crumb tray and empty it out. You can wash it with washing-up liquid (dish soap) and water if it's particularly dirty. Next, turn the toaster upside down and give it a shake over the bin to get out any crumbs. Use a soft-bristled brush or an old toothbrush to gently clean the inside of the toaster slots and remove any stubborn crumbs or debris. Be careful not to damage the heating elements or any other parts inside the toaster. Finally, wipe down the exterior of the toaster with a cloth soaked in vinegar and dry it thoroughly. With these few easy steps, your toaster will look and function like new!

DESCALING THE KETTLE

Did you know that Brits consume around 100 million cups of tea every day?! And we don't just 'pop the kettle on' for a cuppa; we use them for everything from cooking pasta to making gravy and soup. It's no wonder we love our kettles so much! However, we often neglect to show them the love they deserve. So, if you want your beloved kettle to last longer and avoid any unwanted particles in your hot drinks, make sure to descale it every month. After all, a clean kettle is a happy kettle!

Fill your kettle up to three-quarters of its capacity with a mixture of equal parts white vinegar and water. Close the lid properly and bring the kettle to a boil. After that, leave the kettle to soak overnight. Remember to unplug the kettle and put a note on it so no one uses it accidentally. The next day, the limescale will come off easily. Give it a quick wipe and thoroughly rinse the kettle to remove any remaining vinegary odours, then boil fresh water to enjoy your newly descaled kettle!

THE EASY WAY TO REMOVE TEA/COFFEE STAINS

Speaking of a cuppa, when serving a warm cup of tea or coffee to your guests, the last thing you want is to offer them a cup that has brown stains in it. Tannins, which are plant compounds found in tea and coffee, are the main culprits behind cup stains. While tannin stains are not harmful, they can be unsightly and difficult to remove, depending on the type of dishware and the duration of the stain.

To remove the stain, simply drop a denture tablet into your cup and pour in hot water. (You can buy denture tablets from most supermarkets.) Wait for the fizz to die down and let it settle for about five minutes. After that, use a damp cloth or sponge to give it a good scrub and wipe away the stain. You'll find that it comes off fairly easily. Finally, wash your mug using washing-up liquid or put it in the dishwasher as usual.

KEEP THE TOPS OF YOUR CUPBOARDS CLEAN

Let's face it, cleaning the tops of your cupboards is no fun. They are difficult to reach and often collect grime and dust. However, there is a simple solution to make this chore a little less frequent. By lining the tops of your cupboards with newspaper, you can easily remove the paper and replace it with fresh sheets when it gets dirty, saving you time and energy in the long run. This hack is a great way to keep your kitchen looking clean and tidy without the hassle of constantly climbing up to dust the tops of your cabinets.

GIVE YOUR CUTLERY A BATH

There's nothing worse than sitting down to a wonderful meal with cutlery that's dull. A set table at a dinner party with water spots, dried-on food and rust on the knives and forks can be a distraction. Clean and shiny cutlery can add so much to the overall dining experience.

A simple and effective hack for getting your cutlery looking sparkling new again is to line the bottom of a large saucepan with aluminium foil, making sure that the shiny side is facing up. Then, arrange your cutlery on top of the foil, making sure that the knives and forks are not stacked on top of each other. Sprinkle a generous amount of baking soda over the cutlery and pour boiling water over everything until the cutlery is fully submerged. For every 4 litres (1 gallon) of water, use about 1½ tablespoons of baking soda. Bring the mixture to a boil and let it simmer on the hob for around 15 minutes. After that, remove the cutlery using tongs and place it on a paper towel to cool down. If your silverware is heavily tarnished, you may need to repeat the process a few times to get the best results. For larger items, you can use a large baking tray. This trick works like magic and your cutlery will be sparkling clean and ready for your next meal!

BATHROOM
HACKS

So, your bathroom is starting to smell like a university campus after a crazy party? Don't worry, I won't judge. Is there anything worse than a smelly bathroom? (Spoiler alert: nope, there is not.) It can be embarrassing, especially when you have guests over. Surprisingly, though, the bathroom is probably my favourite room to clean. The process of deep cleaning your bathroom isn't as complicated as you might think. Once you get into a groove, you can pretty much tackle the tasks quite quickly to make every inch of your bathroom sparkling and germ-free. Whether you have a shower room, a large en-suite bathroom or just a simple toilet, you still need to rid the areas of lurking germs, soap scum, limescale and more. With my simple tips and tricks, you can get your bathtub, shower and toilets looking so spotless that you'll want to throw a party in there. (If that's your kinda thing... Hey, I said, no judgement!)

Use a Dish Brush for Easy Cleaning

It turns out dish brushes are not only reserved for your dirty plates and cookware; you can use one to make your bathroom sparkle too. Dish brushes are designed to clean off stubborn baked-on grease. There are a few different types – some with bristles, some with a sponge, and some even have scrapers.

The brushes work differently depending on the one you have. Sometimes they squirt soap straight from the brush at the push of a button or the liquid slowly releases as you push down on the sponge.

HOW TO USE A DISH BRUSH

When using a dish brush to clean your bathroom, fill up the handle of the brush with antibacterial washing-up liquid (dish soap), or with 125ml (½ cup) of water, 125ml (½ cup) of white vinegar and 60ml (¼ cup) of washing-up liquid (dish soap). Then you can use it to give the sink, tiles, bathtub, shower and shower door a quick clean before rinsing off the cleaner.

Cleaning your shower or bathtub right after you use them is the best way to attack build-up before they get really grimy. You can spend a few minutes quickly scrubbing down your shower door, tiles and bathtub while you're waiting for your hair conditioner to set. I always like to keep a separate dish brush in my bathroom cupboard for quick access.

Remove Watermarks from Shower Screens

Shower screens and enclosures are important for protecting your bathroom from water damage, but they can also add a stylish touch to your space. To keep your shower glass looking its best, you can use a simple DIY cleaning solution made with water and white vinegar (see page 27). Just pour 125ml (½ cup) of each into a 250ml spray bottle, then spray the solution directly onto the shower screen and rinse it off. For stubborn stains, you can spray a cloth and scrub the area gently, being careful not to damage the glass. Once you're done cleaning, use a squeegee to remove any excess water from the screen. This solution is an effective way to eliminate watermarks and limescale from your shower door or screen, leaving it with a streak-free shine.

Soak Shower Heads in Vinegar

You can use the hack that we discussed earlier (see page 31) to clean your shower head or bathroom taps. If your shower head is detachable, take it off and soak it in a bowl of vinegar, or, if it's fixed, fill a plastic bag with vinegar and tie it around your shower head or tap overnight. This will naturally break down and remove any grime or limescale build-up, leaving your fixtures clean and shiny.

Clean Your Mirrors and Prevent Fogging

I have a great tip to keep your bathroom mirror clean and clear. Did you know that glycerol (a naturally derived ingredient found in shaving foam) can be used to create a protective coating on the glass to stop it from fogging? Yes, it's true! So go ahead, show those steamy showers who's boss! Simply apply a small amount of shaving foam to a cloth, then wipe it evenly across your mirror. You can use this trick on your shower doors, windscreen or glasses to keep them fog-free too.

Speaking of the bathroom, I always do my make-up in there because it has the best lighting in the house, especially when I'm in a hurry. To get out the door as quickly as possible, I always pop a bit of shaving foam on my mirror before I get in the shower. It's like a little pre-shower ritual, with the added bonus of a fog-free mirror. Who knew shaving foam could be so multi-functional?

Banish Urine Smells

Over time, urine can collect on bathroom flooring and at the base around the toilet, especially with kids and pets around. If not tackled quickly, it can produce an unpleasant odour. Luckily, there is a fun, albeit slightly unorthodox, way to clean it up!

To banish the urine smell in your bathroom, grab that trusty can of shaving foam again and apply it to the bottom of the toilet and on the floor surrounding the toilet. After leaving the foam to sit for a few hours, simply wipe it away and you'll have a fresh-smelling bathroom. This trick actually works by drawing out the urine and neutralising the ammonia in it. I know it sounds bizarre, but trust me on this one, it's a game-changer. Shaving foam is a commonly available household item, but for those who don't already own a can, it's pretty inexpensive and you can purchase it at your local supermarket or pharmacy.

Freshen Up with Essential Oils

To add a pleasant aroma to your bathroom, you can pour five drops of your favourite essential oil onto the inside of your cardboard toilet-paper roll. This will create a subtle and pleasant scent in the bathroom. If you don't have essential oil, you can use a concentrated disinfectant like Zoflora as a substitute. Simply pour onto cotton wool and rub it on the inside of the toilet-paper roll.

Clean Hard-water Stains with a Pumice Stick

Hard water is basically water that contains high levels of calcium and magnesium. Over time, it can leave stains in your bathroom, especially in toilet bowls, which hold standing water. Have you ever had trouble getting rid of those pesky hard-water stains in your bathroom? It can be so frustrating and even embarrassing, right? But don't worry, besties, you're not alone in this. Many areas have hard water, and it definitely doesn't mean you're unclean. If you are struggling with hard-water stains in your toilet bowl, try using a pumice stick. It's abrasive but gentle enough to remove the stains without causing any damage to the porcelain of your toilet bowl. Make sure to wet the stick and the bowl first, and then gently rub the stain until it disappears. Also try making some of magic self-cleaning toilet-bowl bombs – see recipe below.

HOW TO MAKE A TOILET BOMB

Ingredients:

120g (½ cup) baking soda

1 tablespoon of essential oil (use tea tree oil or lavender, as they have disinfecting properties).

50g (¼ cup) citric acid (citric acid is a weak organic acid that is commonly found in citrus fruits such as lemons and oranges. It can be used as a natural and effective cleaning agent. You can purchase citric acid online or in supermarkets.)

Method: Mix the baking soda, essential oil and citric acid together in a glass jar. Slowly stir in warm water until you get a damp consistency that holds its shape when squeezed in your hand. Once you have the mixture ready, measure out at least 1 tablespoon and put it into a silicone mould or ice-cube tray. Leave to dry overnight, then pop the toilet bombs out of the moulds and store them in a glass jar, labelled for future use. When it's time to clean your toilet, drop one of the toilet bombs into the bowl and let the fizzing action do the cleaning work for you. These toilet bombs are effective in removing stains and leaving a fresh, clean smell in the bowl.

Clean and Disinfect Your Toilet Brush

We all know how filthy our toilets can get, but can you imagine how dirty our toilet brushes can be? They are packed with bacteria, so it's important to clean them regularly. Do this by sandwiching the brush under the toilet seat to keep it in place. Then rinse the toilet brush with hot water and spray thoroughly with disinfectant, rotating it so you can spray all sides. Leave it to sit under the seat for 15 minutes to drip dry into the bowl before you put it away. While you are waiting, also give your toilet brush holder a good clean with disinfectant and then rinse.

How to Brighten and Clean Grouting

Grout is like the middle child of bathroom tiles – often overlooked and neglected. But just like any other member of the family, it deserves some attention and care. Over time, dirt, grime and mould can build up in the grout lines, making them look dingy and unsightly. Luckily, I have a simple and effective recipe that will brighten and clean your grouting, bringing it back to life in no time. Here's what you need to do.

Make the grout cleaner recipe below, then apply the paste to the grouting with a toothbrush and let it sit for a few minutes. Next, mix equal parts of hydrogen peroxide and water in a spray bottle, spray the solution over the grouting paste, and let that sit for a few minutes. Then scrub the grouting with a toothbrush and rinse it with warm water.

GROUT CLEANER RECIPE

Ingredients:
120g (½ cup) baking soda
85ml (⅓ cup) hydrogen peroxide (see page 28)
1 tablespoon of washing-up liquid (dish soap)

Method: Mix the baking soda, hydrogen peroxide and washing-up liquid (dish soap) to form a paste, ready to apply directly to the grouting.

Make Your Bathtub Sparkle

Bathtimes are universally popular with our children, aren't they? The splashing, the gliding and the adorable little rubber duckies – oh, bless them. But grown-ups need bathtime too! As adults with bills to pay and children to feed, some of us also crave the luxury of a relaxing bath. For me, there's nothing better than soaking in a warm bath after a long day, am I right? When it's bathtime, I go all out! I'm talking bubbles, muscle soak, candles, music and a face mask. I like to create a spa-like atmosphere. It's more than just a bath for me, it's a chance to de-stress and recharge. But in order to fully enjoy our bathtimes, we need to keep our bathtub clean. A sparkling-clean tub not only looks great, but also helps us relax more, fully knowing we are soaking in a hygienic space.

If you're looking for an easy and inexpensive way to clean your bathtub then look no further than your own kitchen! All you need is some baking soda and washing-up liquid (dish soap). Use a bucket or your hand-held shower to pour hot water all over the tub's surface. Then sprinkle baking soda and a few squirts of washing-up liquid (dish soap) into the tub (if you have a lot of soap scum, let them sit for 10 minutes). I like to keep a jar of baking soda in my bathroom cabinet with a perforated lid for easy sprinkling. Fold a towel or mat on the floor and place it under your knees to provide some support. Then scrub the tub's surface with a non-scratch sponge or brush, and rinse away the suds to reveal a sparkling bathtub. Don't forget to then dry the tub with a cloth. This eco-friendly and multi-use cleaning solution can also be used to clean sinks, tiles and fixtures – without any harsh chemicals. Give it a try and your bathroom will be glistening like diamonds in no time.

Use a Dryer Sheet to Clean Soap Scum

Have you ever thought about what to do with used dryer sheets after doing laundry? Before throwing them away, consider using them to clean soap scum off your shower and sink! These slightly abrasive sheets can work wonders in removing limescale deposits from bathroom tiles, tubs and fixtures. Besides, they have a pleasant smell that adds freshness to your bathroom. All you need to do is moisten a used dryer sheet and use it to wipe the surfaces. Give it a try, and you'll be amazed at how well this simple trick works!

TANYA'S TIP

A quick and easy way to test for soap scum on your bathtub surface is to run your hand over the surface. If you feel any friction or resistance, then it's likely that there is still soap scum residue present. To get rid of it, you should keep cleaning until the surface feels completely smooth.

How to Treat Mould

Black mould is a form of fungi often caused by poor ventilation, which results in excess condensation in the house. Dealing with it can be a real challenge, especially in bathrooms where it tends to accumulate on the ceiling, sealant, grouting and even windows. What's worse is that mould can be dangerous and can cause respiratory problems if left untreated. Black mould is a common problem in bathrooms – I've been there. In my case, I don't have a window in my bathroom, and the high levels of moisture caused by hot showers and baths have led to damp issues. Over the years, I've tried many approaches to tackle the mould problem, and it has been frustrating. To be honest, I've had my fair share of tears and tantrums trying to keep on top of it. However, I have finally found a simple and effective solution that works wonders.

My secret weapon is a spray that I make myself using everyday household items. And let me tell you, it's so easy to make and use, and it keeps mould away – it has been a game-changer for me. It's so effective that I feel compelled to share the recipe here for the sake of all mould victims out there! Just spray the affected areas generously and let it sit for about 30 minutes. Then rinse it off with water and wipe the area dry. You can use this spray once a week to prevent mould from growing in your bathroom.

MOULD SPRAY RECIPE

Ingredients:
125ml (½ cup) white vinegar
125ml (½ cup) water
1 tablespoon of tea tree essential oil

Method: Mix together the vinegar, water and tea tree oil in a glass spray bottle, give it a good shake and voilà! You have a powerful cleaning solution that will keep your bathroom mould-free.

HOW TO KEEP MOULD FROM COMING BACK

Remember that prevention is key, so it's essential to keep your bathroom well ventilated. To stop mould growth, you should try to keep your windows open (if you are lucky enough to have them). If you don't have a window in your bathroom, consider installing a fan to circulate the air and prevent condensation. You can also leave the bathroom door open after using it to help the moisture escape.

Rust Stains on Bathroom Fixtures

Rust is the result of a love triangle between iron, oxygen and moisture. When these three get together, iron oxide is generated, which creates the unsightly and dreaded rust. It's like the ex that refuses to go away, only this time, it's the reddish-brown stain that accumulates on the floor or around the sink when you leave your aerosol cans unattended. This is why rust is commonly found on cans of shaving foam or razor blades, but it is also known to show up uninvited around your shower, sink or toilet bowl. If you're unlucky enough to spot rust in your bathroom, don't panic! You can easily break up this rusty love affair by treating it with some simple cleaning methods. With a little TLC, you'll be able to show that rust who's boss in no time.

If you're not keeping a jar of baking soda in your bathroom by now, you are missing out. If you come across a rusty area, rinse it first and then dust it with baking soda. Let it sit for an hour, and then scrub it with some damp steel wool or a stainless-steel scourer until you remove the rust. This trick can help you keep your bathroom looking clean and shiny. Some bathroom fixtures that may be susceptible to rust are taps, shower heads and towel radiators. However, it's important to refrain from using a scourer on your bathtub, as it can damage the surface. Instead, try scrunching up aluminium foil, dipping it in soapy water and scrubbing on your bathtub to remove the rust.

USE SILICA GEL PACKETS TO REDUCE HUMIDITY

Believe it or not, those tiny little packs of silica gel that you get in a box of new shoes can be pretty useful around your home. These packets are designed to absorb moisture and hold water vapour, making them perfect for storing in your bathroom cabinet to help keep humidity at bay and protect your toiletries from spoiling. You can also store them with your razors to prevent rusting. However, be sure to keep them away from children and pets as they can be a choking hazard.

TANYA'S TIP

You can also use silica gel packets in various other places around your home to prevent moisture damage. They are perfect for storing in your closet, with your shoes, with your tools, and even with important documents. By storing silica gel packets in these places, you can help prevent moisture damage and protect your belongings.

Use a Wet Mop to Clean Tile Walls

Cleaning tile walls is like trying to solve a Rubik's cube while standing on one foot. It's a tricky task that can leave you feeling unbalanced and frustrated. And if you need to use a stepladder in the tub, well, that's like trying to solve that Rubik's cube blindfolded. It's just asking for trouble! Cleaning bathroom tiles is a task that I often neglect and forget about because it is incredibly time-consuming. They can get dirty quickly, especially because a bathroom is an area of the home used every day. Not only can dirt and grime spoil the look of a bathroom, but it is also incredibly unhygienic.

To clean your bathroom tiles easily and quickly, you can use a wet mop like Flash, or Swiffer (if you are in the US). The long handle means you can reach all areas easily, and it is ideal for those with small bathrooms. Simply moisten your mop with water, then directly spray the wall with multi-purpose cleaner (check out page 27 for one of my recipes if you like) and clean with your mop. If your tiles are made of natural stone or cement, make sure to use a non-acidic cleaner that's specially formulated for these materials. After cleaning all the walls, switch out the wet cloth for a dry one, and dry the walls. This will eliminate streaks and leave behind a clean sparkle. The bonus is that the lovely scent fills the whole bathroom.

CHAPTER 4

LIVING ROOM HACKS

The living room is often considered the highlight of your home, as it sets the tone for the rest of the house. When my partner, Konan, and I first started decorating our home, it was the first place we tackled. We figured if we could transform the main room, then all the other rooms would fall into place. We just love spending time in our living room. It's where we cuddle up on the sofa to watch our favourite shows, relax after a long day, exchange our Christmas gifts and host loved ones. But with so much use, it can be difficult to keep the space clean and tidy.

Growing up, my childhood home was always bustling with guests. My mother was the epitome of hospitality, always ensuring everyone was comfortable and well fed. She has a heart of gold and is loved by everyone who knows her. My mum loved entertaining so our house was always filled with people - family members, friends and kids running around. She used to tell me, 'Tanya, you never know who might turn up, so we need to keep the living room clean at all times.' Years later, I find myself just like my mother - always ready to welcome guests with open arms. I guess the apple doesn't fall far from the tree.

As a self-proclaimed hostess with the mostess, I'm always ready to roll out the red carpet for my guests, but I've had my fair share of cleaning mishaps. One time, during a lively games night with friends, disaster struck when my friend accidentally spilt a drink on the carpet. I scrambled to clean it up with whatever I could find, but the stubborn stain just wouldn't budge. Needless to say, I learnt my lesson that day and now always have a trusty carpet cleaner on hand. But that's not the only cleaning debacle I've faced. I once found myself dealing with sticky popcorn splattered all over the sofa while babysitting my niece. It was certainly frustrating at the time, but let's be real, who can stay mad at a cute little face? These experiences have taught me the importance of being prepared for any cleaning situation and, more importantly, they taught me that nothing is unfixable.

Our homes are meant to be lived in and enjoyed, not just for show. It's easy to get caught up in trying to make everything perfect, but sometimes we forget to just relax and enjoy the space we have. So you have a little stain here and there, SO WHAT? It can always be fixed. Remember, it's important to prioritise the things that bring us joy and to spend time with the people we love, rather than getting too caught up in the little things.

Fingerprints, Dust and Smudges on Your TV

Believe it or not, I've had the same ancient television in my living room for just over a decade. It's like a family heirloom, but with more pixels. My brother Rudy passed it down to me as a housewarming gift, and I'm starting to think he got it from the set of *Friends*. But, hey, it still works like a charm, so why upgrade? I'm not one of those people who needs the latest and greatest gadgets. As long as it's streaming my favourite shows, I'm all good. You know what they say: if it ain't broke, don't fix it! Or in my case, if it's ancient, don't replace it! Regardless of how they come to be in our homes, we all take pride in our electronic devices. In today's world, electronic devices have become an essential part of our daily lives and we rely on them for various tasks. Whether it's our phones, laptops or TVs, we use them often. Let's face it, these devices are not cheap, and whether we buy them new or second-hand, we want to make sure they last as long as possible. Cleaning your electronic devices correctly is an important part of maintaining them and protecting them from dust, smudges, fingerprints and streaks. By doing so, you can prolong their lifespan and keep them looking like new.

HOW TO CLEAN YOUR TV

To clean your TV screen, start by turning off the TV and letting it cool down. Then, use a soft microfibre cloth to gently wipe the screen in a circular motion. Avoid using paper towels or rough cloths, as these can scratch the screen. For any smudges and fingerprints, you can also use a solution of equal parts water and white vinegar to lightly dampen the cloth for a deeper clean. Be sure to wring out the cloth well before wiping the screen, and never spray the solution directly onto the screen. Clean the body or panel of your TV with the same solution. Avoid pressing too hard as this can damage your TV. Once clean, remove the moisture with a dry cloth.

TANYA'S TIP

Before cleaning a TV or LED monitor screen, it is important to refer to the manufacturer's manual for specific cleaning instructions. Using a cleaning product or method not recommended by the manufacturer may void the product's warranty. It is always better to be safe than sorry, so take a few minutes to read the manual before cleaning your screen.

Scratches on Wooden Furniture

Over time, wood can develop scratches; it's only natural, considering how often we use our dining tables, coffee tables and other pieces of furniture in our homes. Imperfections on wood can provide age and character, creating a rustic aesthetic. But scratches are less appealing as they can distract from the room as a whole. Luckily, there is a simple solution to diminish the appearance of minor wood scratches that involves using a humble walnut.

If the walnut is in a shell, crack it open and take out a large piece of the nut. Rub it over the scratches and warm the area with friction from your finger, making sure the nut's oil soaks into the wood. Go over the scratch from different angles, and finally, use a soft cloth to buff the area. The natural oils in the walnut can work like a polish and remove the blemish, making the wood look new again. This is a quick and easy hack to improve the appearance of your wooden furniture without having to spend money on costly repairs or replacements.

Upholstery Cleaning

So, for the longest time, I had been dreaming of buying a beautiful beige sofa, but I always hesitated because I was afraid of getting it dirty. I mean, who wouldn't be, right? I was worried that it would be too difficult to keep it clean, especially with a clumsy boyfriend around (don't tell him I said that). However, I eventually decided to take the plunge and treat myself. I often hear people saying that one should not buy light-coloured furniture with kids (or, in my case, boyfriends) in the house. But why should we deprive ourselves of the things we love just because we are afraid of messing them up?

Sofas are one of the most used pieces of furniture in our homes, so it's natural for them to accumulate dirt and stains over time. However, if you happen to spill something on your sofa or notice a stain, don't worry too much. There are a few simple tricks you can try to keep your sofa looking and feeling clean and fresh.

HOW TO CLEAN YOUR SOFA

This unconventional sofa-cleaning hack is one of the new ones I happened to stumble across on TikTok. I was so intrigued that I had to go and try it for myself, and lo and behold, it worked a treat.

1 Start by vacuuming your sofa to remove any loose dirt, debris and pet hair.

2 Mix washing-up liquid (dish soap) and warm water in a bowl and soak a microfibre cloth into the soapy water.

3 Wring out the cloth and wrap it around a medium-sized saucepan lid, tying the opposite corners together to hold it in place.

4 Use the cloth-covered lid to scrub the sofa and go over any stains.

5 Repeat the scrubbing process using a clean cloth to remove any residue.

6 Leave the sofa to dry and it will look as good as new.

Scan the QR code for more.

TANYA'S TIP

It's important to keep in mind that certain types of materials, such as leather, require special cleaning solutions. Also, some cushion covers may be machine washable, so it's best to check your sofa's care guidelines before attempting any cleaning hacks.

HOW TO LOOK AFTER LEATHER

Leather sofas are a popular choice for many homeowners. Not only do they look sleek and elegant, but they're also durable and can last for years with proper care. However, just like any other piece of furniture, leather sofas require regular cleaning to maintain their appearance and condition. This can be a bit tricky, but with the right techniques and products, it can be done easily and effectively. Here are some steps to follow to keep your leather sofa looking great:

1 **Clean the leather:** Begin by mixing equal parts water and white vinegar in a bowl. Apply the solution to a soft, clean cloth and gently rub it onto the surface of the sofa. Work in small sections and make sure to apply the cleaner evenly. Avoid using too much water or solution, as this can damage the leather. Use a clean, damp cloth to remove any excess cleaner and allow the sofa to air-dry.

2 **Condition the leather:** Leather goods such as sofas, jackets, boots or bags can last longer if you take care of them properly. A simple way to do this is by using a quality leather conditioner. It helps to prevent dryness and cracks while restoring the natural shine of the leather. You can easily make a leather conditioner at home to keep your leather looking new and help it last longer – see the recipe overleaf. Conditioning the leather will also help to protect it from future stains and damage.

By following these simple steps, you can keep your leather sofa looking great for years to come. Remember to clean and condition the sofa regularly to maintain its appearance and prevent damage.

DIY LEATHER CONDITIONER

Ingredients:
100g (½ cup) natural beeswax
200g (¾ cup) coconut oil
125ml (½ cup) white vinegar
20 drops of lemon essential oil

Method: Half-fill a saucepan with water, then put a metal or heatproof bowl on top of the saucepan to create a double boiler system. You don't want to melt the solution directly in your saucepan as beeswax is hard to clean off. Simmer the water on the hob and add the beeswax to the bowl. Once the beeswax has melted, stir in the coconut oil, vinegar and lemon essential oil. Mix until blended, pour into a glass container and allow to cool. Once cool, apply the conditioner to the leather evenly and buff it with a clean, dry cloth.

KEEP YOUR SOFA SMELLING FRESH

Picture this: you're lounging on your sofa, enjoying a Netflix binge session, and suddenly an unpleasant odour hits your nose. Your sofa may appear to be clean at first glance, but it could still contain unpleasant smells from prolonged use. Pets sneaking onto the couch and cooking fumes that drift through the house can leave behind strong odours that linger for a long time. Fabric sofas are particularly susceptible to these smells. However, there's no need to worry, as you can try a simple hack to freshen your sofa.

If you use dryer sheets to tumble-dry your laundry, instead of throwing them away afterwards, you can use them to freshen up your sofas and pick up pet hair and lint. Simply rub the dryer sheet over your sofa to leave it smelling clean and fresh. After that, you can put a dryer sheet inside your cushion cover

for an extra boost of freshness. It's a simple hack that can make a big difference, and your nose will thank you for it.

Carpet Spills

So, you've been diligent about enforcing a 'no shoes' policy and banning food from carpeted areas – but alas, accidents happen! Whether it's a coffee spill or a flying gravy boat at Christmas, your carpet may end up with a stain. Carpet is a popular flooring choice in many households for several reasons. It adds warmth, style and cosiness to any room. However, keeping it free of everyday stains can be a challenge. Even homes without kids or pets are prone to occasional coffee and red wine spills. Cleaning carpet stains may seem daunting, but with the right technique and cleaning solution – see my go-to recipe on the next page – stubborn spots can be easily removed.

TANYA'S TIP
Remember, the key to removing any carpet or rug stains is to act quickly. The longer you wait, the harder it is to remove the stain.

DIY CARPET SPOT CLEANER

Ingredients:
2 tablespoons of white vinegar
2 tablespoons of cornflour

Method: Mix the vinegar and cornflour to create a thick paste. Apply the paste over the tough stain and allow it to dry completely. In the case of severe stains, leave the paste for up to 2 days. Once the paste has hardened, carefully remove the residue using a butter knife. Finally, vacuum the affected area thoroughly to ensure that no residue remains. This powerful solution is designed to tackle even the toughest carpet stains by forming a hard paste that clings to the stain, making it easier to remove.

HOW TO REMOVE COMMON CARPET STAINS

Here are my tips for tackling the kinds of stains that can easily occur around the home.

Tea or coffee

Tea and coffee are some of the most commonly consumed beverages in households around the world. However, they can also be the cause of stubborn stains on your carpets. If you spill tea or coffee on your carpet, it's important to act quickly to prevent the stain from setting in. To get coffee or tea stains out of the carpet, use a clean, dry cloth or paper towel to blot up as much of the liquid as possible (be sure to blot gently to avoid spreading the stain further). Then mix a solution of equal parts white vinegar and water and apply it to the stain. Let it sit for about 10 to 15 minutes. Then use a clean, dry cloth or paper towel to blot up the cleaning solution and the stain. Repeat this process until the stain is no longer visible. Use a clean cloth dipped in water to rinse the area thoroughly.

Wine

Wine stains on your carpet can be a nightmare to deal with. However, with the right technique and cleaning solution, you can remove them with ease. The first step is to blot up as much of the wine as possible using a clean cloth or paper towel. Next, to dilute the stain, pour a bit of cold water directly onto the wine stain. Then mix 1 tablespoon of washing-up liquid (dish soap) and 1 tablespoon of white vinegar with 200ml (¾ cup) of cold water. Apply the solution to the stain using a new clean cloth, making sure not to saturate the carpet. Keep using new sections of the cloth to blot the stain, working from the outside in. This is to avoid transferring wine back onto the carpet. Rinse the area with clean water and blot dry. If the stain is still visible, mix equal parts of hydrogen peroxide (see page 28) and water and apply it to the stain. Let it sit for five minutes, then blot dry.

TANYA'S TIP

Remember to always test a small, inconspicuous area of the carpet before applying any cleaning solution to the stain. This is to ensure the cleaning solution does not discolour your carpet. With these simple steps, you can say goodbye to wine stains on your carpet for good!

Chocolate

Isn't chocolate the best?
Not only is it delicious,
but studies show that
eating chocolate can
trigger the release of
endorphins, which
are chemicals in the
brain that make us feel happy
and satisfied. Sounds good to me.

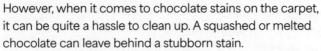

However, when it comes to chocolate stains on the carpet,
it can be quite a hassle to clean up. A squashed or melted
chocolate can leave behind a stubborn stain.

To deal with chocolate stains on your carpet, first, remove
any excess chocolate using a spoon or knife. Be careful not
to spread the stain further. If the chocolate is melted, place
ice cubes over the stain to harden the remaining chocolate
before scraping. Next, mix 200ml (¾ cup) of warm water and
2 tablespoons of washing-up liquid (dish soap). Dip a clean
cloth in the solution, then blot the stain gently – avoid rubbing,
as this can push the stain deeper into the carpet fibres. After
blotting, rinse the area with clean water and blot again to
remove any excess detergent. Then, use a clean, dry cloth to
absorb any remaining moisture. Finally, allow the carpet to dry
completely before walking on it. You can speed up the drying
process by using a fan or opening windows to increase air
circulation.

Wax (or gum)

There's something truly magical about lighting a candle.
The warm glow of the flame can create a cosy and relaxing
atmosphere, instantly transforming a room into a peaceful
sanctuary. Whether I'm winding down after a busy day,
enjoying a relaxing bath or simply reading a good book,
lighting candles has become an essential part of my daily

routine. There's just something about the gentle flicker of the flame that helps me unwind and find a sense of calm in the midst of the chaos of everyday life. Plus, with so many different scents and styles available, I love experimenting with new candles and finding the perfect one to match my mood. Everyone loves the intimate ambience of lighting a candle – that is, until wax drips all over the rug. Luckily, removing wax from your carpet is simple and requires materials that you may already have at home.

To begin with, try to peel away as much wax as you can. Then, use an ice pack to freeze the remaining wax, and once it's frozen, chip it away with a spoon or a dull knife. It's important to vacuum and clean the area thoroughly before the wax softens so that it doesn't get embedded deeper into the carpet fibres. Cover the wax stain with a towel and iron over it on low heat. The wax will be absorbed into the towel, removing the stain. Finally, blot the carpet with a cloth to ensure that all the residue is removed completely. This technique applies to chewing gum as well, so by following these steps, you can tackle wax or gum on your carpet like a pro!

Ink

Ink stains are one of those carpet mishaps that nobody wants to see. Whether it's a leaky biro, or an accident during homework or even by the notorious doodlers among us, an ink stain can be stressful. Did you know that there are two types of ink stains? The first type is water-based, which includes highlighters and magic markers. These stains are temporary and can be dissolved in water, so they're pretty straightforward to remove.

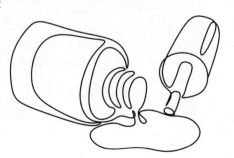

The second type is non-water-based ink, which includes standard ink pens and permanent markers. These stains are usually considered permanent as they are not soluble in water. However, they can still be removed successfully from the carpet with a little extra work.

- **Non-permanent, water-based ink:** Start by blotting up as much of the ink stain as possible using a clean cloth or paper towel. Then, fill a bowl with warm water and add a teaspoon of laundry detergent. Dab the stained area with the solution and repeat until the stain disappears. Finally, rinse the area with water to remove any remaining soapy residue.

- **Permanent ink:** The key here is to act quickly. Start by using a clean cloth or paper towel to blot up as much excess ink as possible. Make sure not to rub the stain, as this can push it further down into the carpet fibres. Once you've removed as much ink as possible, moisten the stain with rubbing alcohol/surgical spirit. Then, using a paper towel, carefully dab the area. You should see the ink transfer onto the paper towel. Keep using a new paper towel each time until the stain is completely gone. Mix a few drops of laundry detergent with warm water and apply to remove any remaining mess, and rinse the area with lukewarm water.
Finally, let the carpet air-dry completely.

TANYA'S TIP

Remember, when dealing with an ink stain, avoid smearing it outwards. This can make the stain worse, so it's important to blot or rub in small movements to keep the stain contained in the already-affected area.

Blood

If you're dealing with a blood stain, the first step is to blot up as much of the fluid as possible. If the blood has already dried, try using an old toothbrush to break up the dried deposit and remove as much as you can. Make a solution by mixing 2 tablespoons of washing-up liquid (dish soap) with 200ml (¾ cup) of cold water, as warm water can cause the blood to clot and become tacky. Dab the mixture onto the stain with a clean cloth, being careful not to rub the stain further into the carpet. You can also pour the solution into a spray bottle and spray the stain before blotting it. Keep sponging the stain with the mixture until it disappears.

Mud and dirt

Mud and dirt are common stains that can easily find their way onto your carpets, especially when it's wet and miserable outside. Dealing with these stains can feel like a never-ending battle. Trust me, I've been there, done that and definitely don't want to do it again on a Friday night before guests arrive! But fear not, because there is a simple solution that can help you remove these stains easily. First, wait for the mud to dry completely to avoid it spreading. Once dry, vacuum as much of it as possible. Then mix a solution of 2 tablespoons of washing-up liquid (dish soap), 100ml (½ cup) of warm water and 100ml (½ cup) of white vinegar. Dip a clean cloth into the solution and then dab the cloth onto the stain. Let the solution sit on the stain for 10 minutes before blotting with a clean cloth or paper towel. Repeat the process until the stain is gone.

Urine

So, your furry best friend has just peed on the carpet and left an unpleasant odour in your home – don't worry! You can easily treat the stain using simple products that you may already have at home. First, absorb as much of the urine as possible using a cloth or paper towel, then mix 100ml (½ cup) of white vinegar with 100ml (½ cup) of water in a spray bottle. To quote Outkast, 'shake it like a Polaroid picture' and spray it on the stain. Let it sit for a few minutes and then blot with a cloth until the area is clean. Keep in mind that the cloth might stink a bit, but, hey, at least you're getting that odour out of your carpet! Next up, grab a can of clear or white shaving foam (don't worry, we're not going to start shaving the carpet – yet). Spread a thin layer of the foam over the damp spot and let it do its magic overnight. Rinse it off the next day with a clean, damp cloth and voilà! Your carpet will be as good as new and both you and your furry friend can now enjoy a fresh-smelling home again.

Make–up

To remove make-up stains from your carpet you should act quickly and avoid rubbing the stain. First, remove any excess make-up using a spoon or a dull knife, or vacuum it up if it's powder. Then pour a small amount of micellar water onto a clean cloth and blot the stain gently. Work from the outside of the stain towards the centre, to avoid spreading the stain further. Continue blotting until the stain is removed, and then rinse the area with warm water and blot it dry with a clean paper towel. Micellar water is a gentle and effective way to remove make-up stains from your carpet, but it's important to test it on a small, inconspicuous area of the carpet first to make sure it doesn't cause any damage or discoloration.

Nail polish

Spilling nail polish on carpets or furniture can be a nightmare. There's no need to panic, but do act quickly – the longer you leave the stain, the harder it is to get out. If the nail polish is still wet, gently blot the excess with a paper towel until nothing comes off. To remove the stain, pour a small amount of nail polish remover onto a clean cloth and gently blot the stain. Avoid rubbing the stain as this can spread it further. If the stain persists, you can try using hairspray or rubbing alcohol (see page 28) to help break down the stain. However, keep in mind that removing nail polish stains is not an easy task and may take some time. Be patient and repeat the process until the stain is gone.

HOW TO KEEP YOUR CARPET SMELLING FRESH

If you're a carpet owner, you know how quickly and easily carpets can fall victim to bad odours. Even though we all love our soft and fluffy floors, let's face it, bad odours can turn your cosy home into a stinky mess. Whether it's your pet's pee or your post-workout funk, those smells can linger and ruin your vibe. But, hey, good job doing those home workouts – I'm here for it! There is no doubt that encountering unpleasant smells in your home can be quite bothersome, but fear not, besties! There's a simple hack to freshen up your carpet and make your home smell like a spa (or at least not like a gym locker).

Mix 200g (¾ cup) of baking soda with 20 drops of essential oil. Pour the mixture into a flour sifter, or a container with a perforated lid, or use a sieve to sprinkle the mixture lightly over your carpet. It's important to break down the mixture as much as possible to avoid damaging your vacuum, which would void your warranty. After sprinkling the mixture onto your carpet, leave it to sit for 30 minutes before vacuuming. Baking soda is a natural deodoriser that absorbs unwanted smells, so you will enjoy a clean and fresh-smelling carpet with an added fragrance boost.

CARPET INDENTATIONS

Oftentimes, just moving furniture around a little bit can be the missing piece we need to give our homes a refreshing new look. However, when you move your furniture, you might notice indentations on your carpet that have been left behind over time. This can also be the case if you move into a new home and find reminders of the previous owner's furniture. If you want to get rid of these indentations once and for all, there is a budget way to restore your carpet. Place an ice cube on top of the indentation and let it melt completely, then use a clean cloth to blot up any excess water. Next, use a spoon or a coin to gently fluff up the fibres of the carpet. You can also use a soft-bristled brush. If the indentation is particularly stubborn, you can repeat the process a few times until the fibres have fully bounced back. With this simple trick, you can enjoy a fresh and clean carpet without any unsightly indentations.

HOW TO FLATTEN A RUG

How frustrating is it when your beautiful new rug keeps curling at the corners? This tends to happen when you lay down a new rug that has been in storage for a while, or even with an old rug over time. Not only does it make the rug look old and worn out, but it can also create a potential tripping hazard. If a rug has just been unrolled, it may simply need a few days to flatten itself out. You can even place heavy objects on the corners, such as furniture or large books, to speed up the process. If there's no luck after a few days, there is a simple hack you can try. Placing a few ice cubes on the area and then holding it flat with a heavy object placed just above the ice can do the trick. Wait until the ice melts, then lift the object away, and your rug should be flat.

TANYA'S TIP

If you want a fast and effective way to keep your rug flat, you can use double-sided carpet tape on the back of it. This will help to smooth out any creases and prevent new ones from forming.

CHAPTER 5

BEDROOM HACKS

Why is the bedroom the designated dumping ground that always gets abandoned on the cleaning list? Or is it just me? It's strange how I often put off cleaning my bedroom, even though I spend roughly a third of my life in that space. It's as if I close the door during the day and ignore the clutter and mess that's accumulated. I keep telling myself that I'll come back to it later, but that later never seems to arrive. Instead, the end of the day rolls around, and I'm too exhausted to deal with the mess, so I put it off until the next day. And so the cycle continues. I try not to be so hard on myself; knowing the rest of the house is tidy almost gives me an excuse or a pass to keep my bedroom a tip. It's all about balance. I know that the condition of my bedroom can have a significant impact on my mental well-being and the quality of my sleep, though, so I want to improve. While it's important to prioritise the non-negotiables and be kind to ourselves, it's also worth considering ways to make the task of keeping our bedrooms clean and tidy less daunting.

Step-by-step Bedroom Clean

Cleaning your bedroom can seem like an overwhelming task, but with a little bit of effort and consistency, you can create a peaceful and relaxing space. The key is to break it down into smaller tasks (focusing on one area at a time) or set aside specific times to tidy up.

First, open the windows, put any clean laundry away, and any dirty washing into the laundry basket. If you're in a rush and need a quick solution to hide clutter, you can put it away in your wardrobe or under the bed. However, if you have some time to spare, it's best to start decluttering your space. Begin by going through your closet and dresser and getting rid of clothes that no longer fit or you haven't worn in a while. You can donate or sell these items to free up space. This not only creates more room, but also makes it easier to find the clothes you want to wear.

Next, clean the mirrors and dust all surfaces, including dressers, nightstands and shelves. Use a microfibre cloth to trap dust particles and avoid spreading them around. Don't forget to dust any decorative items such as picture frames and lamps. Now it's time to tackle the floor. Vacuum or sweep the entire room, paying special attention to corners, under the bed, skirting boards and behind furniture. Cleaning the bedding is also important for maintaining a clean and healthy sleeping environment. Wash your sheets, pillowcases and blankets on a regular basis, following the care instructions on the labels. By following these simple steps, you can maintain a clean and clutter-free bedroom that promotes a good night's sleep and improves your overall health and well-being.

Keeping Your Mattress Clean

Merely changing your bedding won't be enough to maintain a hygienic and sanitised sleeping environment. Cleaning and protecting your mattress is crucial to extend its lifespan and to ensure a healthy sleep environment. It's important to flip and rotate your mattress every three months to prevent uneven wear. Over time, mattresses can also accumulate dust mites, bacteria and allergens that can lead to health problems such as allergies, asthma and skin irritation, so by regularly cleaning and protecting your mattress, you can reduce the chances of these issues occurring and promote better sleep.

TANYA'S TIP

Before you begin cleaning your mattress, it is important to first check the manufacturer's care guide. This is because different types of mattresses require different cleaning methods, so it's essential to see if there are any specific instructions you need to follow. By doing this, you can ensure that you don't accidentally damage your mattress and that you take any necessary precautions.

FRESHEN YOUR MATTRESS

To keep your mattress smelling fresh, you can sprinkle baking soda and a few drops of essential oil evenly over the surface and let it sit for three hours. This will help neutralise any unpleasant odours, while the essential oil will give your mattress a refreshing scent. After three hours, simply vacuum up any remaining powder and enjoy the feeling of a newly refreshed mattress. For better air quality inside your room, open the windows to ventilate it - this will also help freshen up your mattress by allowing it to breathe and start to eliminate any odours.

TANYA'S TIP

It's important to note that some essential oils can be harmful to pets, so if needed, you can omit them (see page 14).

VACUUM YOUR MATTRESS

Similar to how you vacuum carpets, furniture and upholstery, your mattress can also benefit from weekly vacuuming. By removing hair, dust and dead skin cells regularly, you can keep your bed in better condition for longer.

INVEST IN A MATTRESS PROTECTOR

To keep your mattress free from stains, spills and wear and tear, you need to get yourself a mattress protector. It will save you the trouble and expense of replacing your mattress prematurely. With proper care and protection, you can maintain a clean, hygienic and cosy sleep environment for a long time.

MATTRESS STAINS

Mattress stains are a common issue that many people face, and some of the most common types are blood, sweat and urine. You should always try to tackle any stains as soon as they occur. Using a gentle laundry detergent or 2 tablespoons of washing-up liquid (dish soap) mixed with 200ml (¾ cup) of lukewarm water is the best way to remove these stains. However, if it's a blood stain, it's recommended to use cold water instead of lukewarm water. When removing stains from your mattress, remember not to rub the stain as it can cause further damage. Instead, gently dab the stain with a cloth to lift the stain as much as possible. Also, avoid using too much water as this can damage the foam and fillings inside your mattress. Make sure the cloth is only damp, not dripping wet. Once you've removed the stain, leave your mattress to air-dry before putting your sheets back on. This will ensure that the mattress is completely free of any moisture that could lead to mould or mildew growth.

CHAPTER 6

WALLS, WINDOWS AND OTHER AREAS

It's common to clean your sink and countertops regularly, but what about the other areas of your home that are often overlooked, such as walls or windows? In this section, I will be providing tips and tricks to help you create a beautiful and functional space by exploring ways to make the most of every inch of your home. I will also be sharing techniques to cut down on cleaning time for areas such as floors that we may do regularly.

The goal is to ensure that your living space is not only aesthetically pleasing, but also comfortable and practical. Let's dive in and discover how to transform these often-neglected areas into stunning features that will elevate the overall look and feel of your home.

Cleaning Your Walls

Raise your hand if as a child you ever dreamt of cleaning your walls. Anyone? No? I didn't think so. Cleaning your walls is like eating sprouts – nobody wants to do it, but it's good for you. Most of us often overlook the importance of cleaning our walls, even though we touch and lean against them daily. It's just as crucial as cleaning other household surfaces, such as mopping the floors and vacuuming the rugs. While it may not be the most exciting task, a little bit of investment in the walls of your abode can make a big difference to the overall appearance of your home. Dust, cobwebs, stains, scuffs, fingerprints and dirt are just a few of the things that can accumulate on your walls over time, but fear not, my fellow wall-cleaning procrastinators, I have a few simple tips that will make this task a breeze.

CLEANING PAINTED WALLS

When washing painted walls, it's important to first consider the type of finish. The finish of the paint, whether it be glossy or matte, will determine how scrubbing will affect the appearance of the wall.

Different types of paint finishes

- **Flat or matte** finishes do not reflect light and have a dull, chalky appearance. These finishes do not hold up well to scrubbing, so extra care should be taken when cleaning walls with a matte finish.

- **Satin** finishes, also known as eggshell finishes, are shinier and more durable than flat finishes.

- **Semi-gloss** finishes are even stronger and have more sheen than satin finishes, making them resistant to wear and tear from cleaning.

- **High-gloss** finishes are the most reflective and are tough against stains; they are usually found on external doors and in bathrooms. They can endure scrubbing when you're cleaning the walls.

SPOT–CLEANING WALLS

So, you have mucky fingerprints on your walls from your young kids, splashes of mud from your dog, and grease splatters from vigorously cleaning those pots and pans. It sounds like a fun house! What's the point in having a home if we don't make good use of it, right? However, we can all get better at giving our walls a good clean now and again to preserve that freshly painted look. A great tip to spot clean your wall surfaces is to use a damp white microfibre cloth dipped in baking soda. The baking soda provides abrasion that helps to remove the stains effectively. However, it's important to test this method on an inconspicuous area first to ensure it doesn't damage the surface.

DEEP–CLEANING WALLS

You should aim to deep clean your walls around once a year. A good time to do this is during a big spring-cleaning session. Start by dusting off any excess dirt using a cloth-covered broom or dry microfibre mop. This will prevent dirt and grime from being smeared around. Always test your cleaning products in an inconspicuous area, such as behind your furniture, as some paint can be damaged by cleaning. To clean your walls, fill a bucket with warm water and add a tablespoon of washing-up liquid (dish soap). Next, take a soft sponge mop, microfibre cloth, or a mop covered in a cloth, and dip it in the cleaning solution. Make sure to wring out as much water as possible from the mop, as too much liquid could result in water stains being left on your walls. Use your mop to work your way from left to right, top to bottom, in a 'W' shape. After cleaning, wipe the wall with a dry microfibre mop to avoid water stains. Always use soft sponges and cloths to avoid scratching the paintwork.

GREASY WALL STAINS

When it comes to removing greasy stains from walls, a tried-and-tested method is to use white vinegar. Simply mix 200ml (¾ cup) of white vinegar and 200ml (¾ cup) of warm water in a bucket, and use a soft sponge to tackle stubborn stains. For glossy paint finishes that require a gentler touch, try rubbing a generous amount of chalk onto the stained area until it is fully covered. Then, use paper towels or tissue paper to wipe off the chalk and follow up with a damp cloth. You'll be left with a sparkling-clean wall without any damage to the paint.

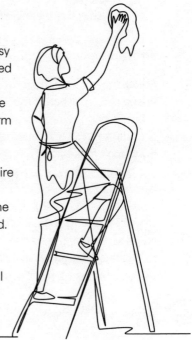

Skirting Boards

When cleaning skirting boards, avoid the temptation to wipe them with a mop. This will leave dust sticking to them, making them look unsightly. Instead, use a vacuum (with a brush attachment if you have one) to hoover up all the dirt. After that, dust your skirting boards with a dryer sheet or a dry microfibre cloth and then go over them with a damp microfibre cloth.

Windows

Cleaning windows can be a real (*ahem*) pane in the glass, especially if you're hoping for a streak-free shine. I must admit that I tend to avoid some household tasks, such as cleaning the oven. But here's a confession – I actually enjoy window cleaning. I know, I know, it's a weird quirk of mine. I remember when I was in school and the window cleaners would come in, I would just stare at the windows, fascinated by the process. We all have our little foibles, and there's no judgement here. One of my guilty pleasures is going online and watching window-cleaning videos, which I find quite satisfying. So, if you need any tips or just want to geek out with me over window cleaning, I'm your gal. However, it did take me a few attempts before I perfected my window-cleaning technique. There are several factors to consider, such as the products, tools, timing and weather conditions, before embarking on this task. So, let's get started and get those windows gleaming!

1 **Brush down your windows**. To clean your windows effectively, start by using a soft-bristled brush like the one that comes with a dustpan-and-brush set. Begin with a thorough brushing

to remove any dirt, cobwebs or debris from both the inside and outside of the windows. It's important to remove as much dust as possible before cleaning with water, as wet dust is much harder to clean off.

2 **Clean your windows with soapy water**. Mix 400ml (1¾ cups) of warm water with 100ml (½ cup) of white vinegar and 2 teaspoons of washing-up liquid (dish soap) in a bucket. Next, soak a cloth in the solution, wring it out and use it to wipe your windows clean. For high windows, wrap the cloth around a flat mop with an extended handle. Be sure to cover the entire surface of the window evenly while cleaning, including the frames and sills. Remember to clean your windows on a cloudy day, as direct sunlight can cause the cleaning solution to dry too quickly and leave streaks.

3 **Use a squeegee for a streak-free shine**. Starting at the top of the window, use a squeegee to remove the cleaning solution. Use a back-and-forth motion, applying firm pressure and wiping the blade after each stroke. Make sure to overlap each stroke slightly to avoid leaving streaks. After you've finished, use a microfibre cloth to wipe down the window surface. Make sure to dry the edges and corners thoroughly to avoid water spots. Finally, use a clean cloth to wipe down the window frames and sills. Make sure to remove any excess water or cleaning solution.

4 **Polish your windows with vinegar**. As the last step, pour 125ml (½ cup) of vinegar and 125ml (½ cup) of water into a 250ml spray bottle and spray it directly onto the glass and polish with a glass and mirror cloth. These cloths don't scratch surfaces and are usually lint-free.

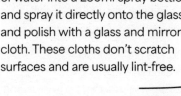

Mop with Cleaner Water

If you're someone who likes to work smarter, not harder when it comes to cleaning, then you know the importance of finding efficient cleaning hacks. This is especially true when it comes to mopping. It can be frustrating to dip your mop into a bucket, only to find that the water becomes murky after mopping just one room. Having to change the water for each room can be time-consuming and costly, but what if I told you that there is a simple solution to this problem that won't break the bank?

All you need is a mop bucket with a wringer, a smaller bucket or container, some water and your chosen floor cleaner. Place the smaller bucket inside the empty mop bucket; I often use a bin-like container to get a good surface area for the mop to slot into. Fill the smaller container with the water and floor cleaner (according to the product's instructions). Dip your mop into the smaller container and clean your floors as usual, then rinse the mop in the wringer of your mop bucket. The dirty water will rinse out of the mop and into the larger bucket, leaving the water in the container clean. This way, you're using cleaner water to mop your floors, and you won't have to change the water after each room. This hack will save you both time and money in the long run. Give it a try, and you'll be amazed at how much easier and more efficient your mopping routine becomes.

Mop with Cleaner Water

Dealing with Dust

I have always been particular about keeping my home clean and tidy, but dusting was one of the chores that I dreaded the most. As someone who suffers from asthma, dusting my home has always been a challenging task. Every time I would start dusting, I would end up coughing and wheezing, making it difficult to breathe. I had tried to keep on top of dusting, but as soon as I had finished dusting one area, I would notice a layer of dust settling on another surface. I tried everything from feather dusters to vacuuming with special attachments, but nothing seemed to work well enough to alleviate my symptoms.

Then one day, I stumbled upon a new dust-repellent recipe that would keep dust away for longer (see recipe below). I was sceptical at first but decided to give it a try. To my surprise, it worked really well. Now, I make a point of dusting my home regularly using a few tried and true methods that have helped alleviate my asthma symptoms, so I no longer dread this task. Dust is just one of those things that keeps coming back whether we like it or not, but fear not, as there are a few simple hacks you can try to keep it at bay.

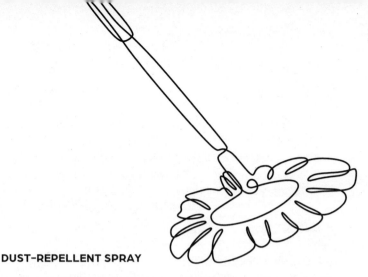

DUST-REPELLENT SPRAY

You can create a magical dust-repellent spray at home to keep dust away for a longer period of time using the recipe below. Simply pour the ingredients into a spray bottle and use it to wipe down all dust-prone surfaces, such as coffee tables, skirting boards and behind the TV. The coating left by the spray helps prevent dust from sticking to surfaces, making it easier for you to clean those hard-to-reach areas. However, keep in mind that this spray is not a miracle worker, and you will still need to dust your shelves and furniture eventually. But, by using this spray regularly, you can reduce the frequency of dusting and it also leaves your home smelling fresh and clean.

MAKE YOUR OWN DUST-REPELLENT SPRAY

Ingredients:
140ml (½ cup) water
70ml (¼ cup) white vinegar
2 tablespoons of olive oil
10 drops of essential oil

Method: Mix the water, vinegar, olive oil and essential oil in a 250ml spray bottle. Give it a shake and use it in place of your regular surface cleaner for better results.

USE A LINT ROLLER

To ensure that every nook and cranny is clear of dust, try using a lint roller to clean fabric surfaces such as lampshades and bed headboards. Unlike traditional feather dusters, this hack collects even the smallest particles without spreading them around.

DUST WITH A DRYER SHEET

An easy and effective way to repel dust is by using a dryer sheet. I always save the dryer sheets from doing my laundry to dust my skirting boards and lampshades. Using this method lessens the frequency of dusting and leaves my home with a nice fragrance too. Happy dusting!

CHAPTER 7

PERSONAL ITEMS

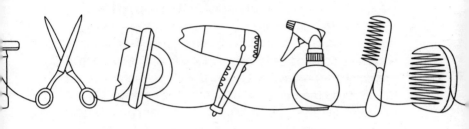

Welcome to the chapter where we'll be scrubbing clean all those everyday items that live in your bathroom, on your dressing table or in your handbag. Think of it as giving them a much-needed spa day, where we'll be getting rid of all the dirt, grime and bacteria that may have accumulated over time. And just as a spa day rejuvenates your mind and body, cleaning your personal items will make them look and feel brand new and ready for use. From your hairbrush to your toothbrush, and from your make-up brushes to your jewellery, here you'll find easy and effective cleaning tips that will help you keep your intimate items clean and germ-free. So, let's get started and give these essential tools the TLC they deserve!

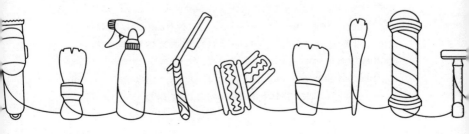

Give Your Hairbrush a Bath

A hairbrush or comb can accumulate oil, dirt, dead skin cells and hair products pretty quickly, leading to a build-up of unwanted residue in your hair. Therefore, it is important to clean them regularly to prevent all that gunk getting back into your hair. To clean your hairbrush or comb, fill your sink with warm water and add 2 tablespoons of baking soda and a few drops of shampoo. Stir the water well and then submerge the entire plastic brush or comb in the water, letting them soak for 30 minutes. However, it is important to be careful with wooden brushes and not to submerge them entirely in water, as it could damage the wood and finish. Instead, only submerge the bristles. For brushes that are very dirty, you can use an old toothbrush to clean the base and bristles. With these simple steps, your hairbrush or comb will be squeaky clean and ready to use, leaving you with beautiful, healthy hair.

Sanitise Your Toothbrush and Holder

It's completely normal to be concerned about the cleanliness of your toothbrush. After all, we use it every day to keep our mouths clean and healthy. I don't know about you, but the thought of putting a toothbrush in my mouth that's crawling with germs petrifies me. So, let me tell you a secret – denture tablets aren't just for your grandparents! You can also use them as a toothbrush sanitiser. Just pop one tablet in a jar of warm water and wait until it fully dissolves. Soak your toothbrush in the jar for 15 minutes and voilà! Your toothbrush will be cleaner than your conscience after a week of kale and green smoothies. Lastly, give your toothbrush a good rinse with water and wipe it dry. Don't forget to give your toothbrush holder some love too; it's like a little home for your toothbrush, and we wouldn't want it to get mouldy and smelly. To clean the holder, place a denture tablet inside with some water and wait for it to dissolve, then scrub it clean with an old toothbrush and rinse it with water. Your toothbrush holder will be as good as new!

Make-up Brushes

Cleaning your make-up brushes can be a tiresome task that many of us neglect. However, not washing our brushes can lead to an accumulation of make-up, oil, bacteria and dirt, which can cause skin problems such as acne, blackheads and clogged pores. No, thank you, ma'am! Therefore, it's crucial to keep our brushes clean, not only for the health of our skin, but also for smoother make-up application. Clean brushes ensure that we look our best and feel like the fabulous divas we are. Yes, please!

To clean your make-up brushes effectively, start by wetting the bristles with warm water. It is important to hold each brush facing downwards to prevent water from seeping into the base, as this can weaken the glue and cause the bristles to come loose. Next, gently cleanse the brush using soap and allow it to lather. You can use the palm of your hand or a brush-cleaning glove or pad, swirling the brush on the surface to remove any dirt or grime. Silicone cleaning tools with small raised bumps are particularly helpful in loosening solidified make-up from brushes.

After cleaning, rinse brushes thoroughly with warm water until the water runs clear. Squeeze out the excess by pressing the bristles gently to release any remaining moisture. Avoid leaving your brushes upright as it can ruin their shape. Instead, lay them flat on a clean towel overnight to air-dry.

TANYA'S TIP

To keep your brushes in good shape, use rubber bands to tie them to the bottom of a clothes hanger to dry. Make sure to attach them so the bristles are facing down. This will help them maintain their shape, and allow air to circulate around the bristles. Once the brushes are dry, they will be ready for use the next morning!

Jewellery

After some time, your jewellery may lose its shine and appear dull. However, you don't need to break the bank on fancy jewellery cleaners to revive your favourite pieces. With some budget-friendly ingredients that you likely already have at home, you can easily restore your rings, earrings, necklaces and other jewellery to their former glory.

TANYA'S TIP

If your jewellery is significantly tarnished or contains delicate gemstones, it may not withstand cleaning methods that are designed for other types of jewellery. It is important to know exactly what your jewellery is made of. If you are uncertain, it is best to err on the side of caution and have your jewellery examined by a professional.

TARNISHED SILVER

When it comes to cleaning sterling silver and silver-plated jewellery, it's useful to note that these have a lower percentage of silver than solid silver and are therefore more likely to tarnish. One effective way to clean them is to line a bowl with aluminium foil. Place your jewellery in the bowl, then fill it with boiling water and 2 tablespoons of baking soda, and stir until bubbles form. Let it sit for up to five minutes until the bubbles have stopped, then carefully remove the jewellery with tongs, rinse with cold water, and dry thoroughly with a soft cloth. Your jewellery will be shiny and sparkly in no time!

TANYA'S TIP

To check if your jewellery is sterling silver, look for markings on the clasp that say 9.25, 925/1000, Sterling, S/S or Sterling 9.25. If you don't see any of these markings, it's likely that your necklace or bracelet is silver-plated. Alternatively, use a magnet on your jewellery; if it sticks, it's likely silver-plated.

GOLD JEWELLERY

To clean your gold jewellery, begin by soaking it in 200ml (¾ cup) of warm water mixed with 1 tablespoon of washing-up liquid (dish soap) for a few minutes. Then, use a soft-bristled toothbrush to gently scrub the surface of your jewellery. Be sure to get into all the nooks and crannies where dirt and grime can accumulate. Rinse your jewellery thoroughly with warm water and dry it with a soft, lint-free cloth. Avoid using harsh chemicals or abrasive materials that can scratch the surface of your gold jewellery. With proper care and maintenance, you can maintain its shine and beauty for years to come.

House and Car Keys

To clean your keys, begin by wiping them down with a damp microfibre cloth to remove any surface dust or debris. Next, mix a small amount of washing-up liquid (dish soap) with warm water in a bowl. Dip a soft-bristled toothbrush into the soapy water and gently scrub your keys, paying special attention to the crevices and hard-to-reach areas. Once you've cleaned your keys thoroughly, rinse them off with warm water and dry them with a clean towel. For extra protection against germs, you can also sanitise your keys by cleaning them with a disinfectant wipe or spray and letting them air-dry. Don't get your keys too wet, though, as excess moisture can damage the electronic components of car keys.

Glasses and Sunglasses

Glasses are susceptible to getting dirty and smudged, which can compromise their effectiveness. Cleaning your glasses regularly not only ensures that they remain in good condition, but also helps to improve your vision. First, rinse them in lukewarm water. Then use a lens cleaner, or mix equal parts of water and rubbing alcohol (see page 28) in a spray bottle to make your own cleaner. Don't use hot water or soap, as they can damage the lenses and the coating. Use a microfibre cloth to wipe down the lenses and frame. Avoid using paper towels or tissues as they can scratch the coating on your glasses. They also leave behind residues that can attract dust and dirt. When not in use, store your glasses in a protective case and avoid placing them face down on hard surfaces or exposing them to extreme temperatures. Cleaning your glasses might seem like a simple task, but it requires a bit of finesse to ensure that you do not damage them.

CHAPTER 8

CLEANING GADGETS AND TOOLS

As someone who loves cleaning, I have found that using cleaning gadgets can make the task even more enjoyable and efficient. I have experimented with various cleaning tools and have come up with a list of some of my favourites. My followers often reach out to me for recommendations, so here is a guide to some of the best cleaning gizmos I have come across.

Squeegee

A squeegee is a useful tool with a rubber blade that effectively removes or controls liquids on various surfaces, leaving them streak-free and clean. While it is commonly used for cleaning windows, it can also be used on other surfaces such as tiles, mirrors, shower doors and car windscreens. Personally, I find this tool particularly helpful in the bathroom. If you want to keep it clean and free from soap-scum build-up, take two minutes after every shower to wipe down your tiles, tub and shower screen with a squeegee to quickly remove water and condensation from these surfaces. This simple habit can save you a lot of time and effort in the long run, as you won't have to clean your bathroom as often. So, if you don't already have a squeegee in your shower, it's time to invest in one!

Robotic Vacuum Cleaner

Robot vacuum cleaners are autonomous devices that use various sensors and algorithms to navigate and clean floors in a home or office. These little robots are a game-changer when it comes to keeping floors clean. They can be programmed to clean at specific times even when you are not at home and can navigate around furniture with ease.

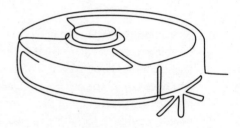

Steam Cleaner

These are devices that use high-temperature steam to clean and sanitise surfaces. Unlike traditional cleaning methods that use chemicals and detergents, steam cleaners harness the power of water vapour to remove dirt, grime and bacteria from floors, carpets, upholstery and even kitchen appliances. They are effective at removing stubborn stains and eliminating germs without leaving any residue or harmful chemicals behind. Steam cleaners are also eco-friendly and cost-effective, since you don't need to buy cleaning agents or disposable cleaning tools. Overall, they are an excellent choice for anyone looking for a safe, efficient and sustainable way to keep their home or workplace clean and healthy.

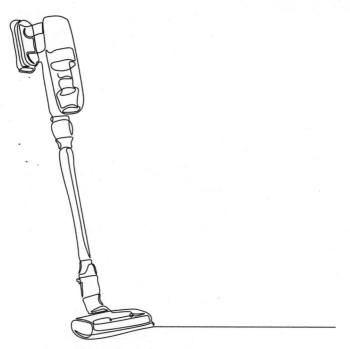

Cordless Vacuum

Cordless vacuums work by using a rechargeable battery to power the motor. These lightweight vacuums are perfect for quick clean-ups and are easy to manoeuvre around the house. They are also great for reaching tight spaces and corners.

Electric Scrubber

This is one of my favourite cleaning gadgets. Honestly, I don't know what I did before I started using one. It is a complete game-changer. It's excellent for cleaning grout, bathtubs, sinks, taps, ovens and many other surfaces. With different attachments for specific cleaning tasks, it can be a real time- and space-saver. My favourite feature of the electric scrubber is the extension rod that allows you to lengthen the handle. It's great for cleaning hard-to-reach places without bending or kneeling, which is also perfect if you are pregnant, disabled, elderly or recovering from an injury.

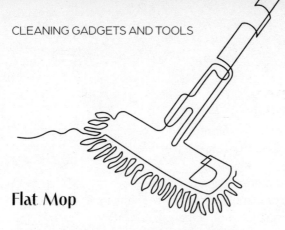

Flat Mop

Flat mops such as the Flash Speed Mop or Swiffer are a cleaning tool that can help make household cleaning tasks much easier. They are lightweight and easy to use, making them a great choice for people who want to keep their homes clean without expending too much time or effort. Flat mops are particularly useful for cleaning hard floors, such as tiles, laminate and hardwood, and they come with disposable pads (wet and dry) that can be easily replaced when they become dirty or worn. You can also get mops with reusable pads, which you can pop in the washing machine. These flat mops can be used to clean floors, tiles, windows, blinds, mirrors, ceilings, walls, plants and more.

Spin Mop

Spin mops are a popular cleaning tool that have gained a lot of attention in recent years. They consist of a bucket with a built-in wringer and a mop head that spins around when you push down on a pedal. The spinning motion helps to remove excess water from the mop head, making it easier to clean your floors without leaving them soaking wet. Spin mops are a great choice for those who want to clean their floors quickly and efficiently, without having to constantly wring out a traditional mop. They are also more hygienic, as the spinning motion helps to remove dirt and grime from the mop head, preventing it from spreading bacteria around your home. With their ease of use and effectiveness, spin mops are definitely worth considering for your next cleaning session.

Hob Scrapers

Hob scrapers remove burnt-on food, grime and residue from your hob or stove. They are typically made of metal or plastic and come in different shapes and sizes to fit various types of hobs. Hob scrapers are great because they can easily remove stubborn stains without damaging the surface of your hob. Unlike scouring pads, hob scrapers are gentle on your hob and don't leave any scratches or marks. They are also reusable, making them an eco-friendly choice for cleaning. With the regular use of a hob scraper, your hob will look shiny and new.

Microfibre Cloths

These cloths are incredibly versatile and can be used for a wide range of cleaning tasks. They are also reusable, making them an eco-friendly option.

TANYA'S TIP

Here's a helpful tip for disinfecting your microfibre cloths ahead of the spring clean. Once a year, you can fill a large pot with water and baking soda, and boil your cloths on the stove for 15 minutes. Pour out the water safely and once the cloths have cooled down, you can wash them in the machine as normal. It's worth noting that some people do this for their laundry, but it's not recommended, as it can shrink your clothes.

Toothbrushes

Old toothbrushes can be the perfect little tool for cleaning in all those nooks and crannies, such as grouting between tiles, window and shower tracks, tap areas, sink drains and even under the toilet rim. They are a great resource for repurposing and reusing and are easily available.

These are just a few of the many cleaning gadgets and tools available on the market. Experiment with different ones and find the ones that work best for you and your cleaning routine. I always keep a list of my favourite cleaning gadgets and products on my Amazon storefront. You can find this on my website or social-media pages.

CHAPTER 9

BONUS CLEANING TIPS

As someone who has struggled with maintaining a clean and clutter-free environment, I know first-hand how overwhelming it can be to get out the mop and the cleaning products and tackle the task of cleaning. However, I have gained some valuable insights over the years that have made cleaning easier and even enjoyable for me. So I would like to share these additional tips and tricks I've learnt along the way, which can help you keep your living space clean, organised and stress-free. By incorporating these hacks into your life, you will save time and energy, and also create a healthier and happier living environment for yourself. So, let's jump in and explore my bonus cleaning tips!

Breaking Down Tasks

When you look at your entire living space as one giant task, it can be easy to feel like you're in a continuous cleaning loop. Instead, try breaking down the workload into smaller, more manageable parts. This can help you approach cleaning without feeling overwhelmed. If you treat house-cleaning like a marathon, you may come to associate it with the stress and tedium that accompanies it. You'll be surprised at how quickly you can get things done when you're not worrying about the big picture. So, don't let cleaning get you down! Just take it one task at a time and you'll be done before you know it.

'Don't Put It Down, Put It Away'

'Ah, that old chestnut,' I hear you say! But if you want to keep your home or workspace tidy, this simple mantra will help you avoid clutter build-up.

The premise is that all the items you own should have a home. That doesn't mean everything needs to be hidden away, but neither does your coffee table have to be a dumping ground. It's easy just to put things down, but it's not that difficult to store them away in their home. Keeping a place tidy can really be that simple.

How often have you spent precious time looking for your phone or keys? If your house is messy and cluttered, it will be difficult to find the things you need, and this wasted time can really add up – which makes those extra few seconds it might take to put something away start to look like a pretty good use of your time.

The Sunday Reset Hack

This hack is as simple as dedicating an hour every Sunday to work on your home. By doing this, you can set yourself up for a successful week ahead. Trust me, you'll be slaying your entire week if you do this right. The Sunday reset involves completing tasks such as cleaning out your refrigerator, mopping your floors, doing a laundry load, changing your bed sheets and preparing anything you need for Monday morning. Don't forget to do something nice for yourself as well. If you consistently follow the Sunday reset, not only will it give you a sense of accomplishment, it'll also make your Monday mornings a lot less chaotic. And who knows? You might just inspire others to join the trend too!

To help you get started, here are some examples of tasks that you could add to your Sunday reset list. Choose a few and use the empty checklist on the next page to create your own list:

SUNDAY RESET CHECKLIST

- Change your bedding
- Do your laundry
- Clear out your fridge
- Water your plants
- Do some light exercise
- Tidy up
- Mop your floors
- Create a food-shopping list
- Meal prep for the week
- Charge all electronics
- Plan your week ahead
- Do a full skincare routine
- Treat yourself
- Take time to rest
- Journal for five minutes
- Read a book
- Meditate
- Take downtime from social media

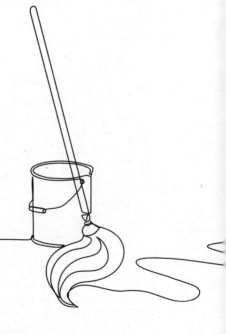

SUNDAY RESET CHECKLIST

- [ ] _____
- [ ] _____
- [ ] _____
- [ ] _____
- [ ] _____
- [ ] _____
- [ ] _____
- [ ] _____
- [ ] _____
- [ ] _____
- [ ] _____
- [ ] _____
- [ ] _____
- [ ] _____

CHAPTER 10

SCHEDULES AND CHECKLISTS

Schedules and checklists can make or break your productivity. You either love them or you hate them; they either work for you or they don't. Personally, I have a schedule and checklist for just about everything in my life - from cleaning and shopping to work, finances and health appointments. It helps me stay organised, motivated and less stressed. Plus, I have the memory of a goldfish, so writing things down is a must. Being able to tick off completed tasks gives me a sense of accomplishment and satisfaction.

Let me share a funny little story with you about how I discovered the magic of cleaning schedules and checklists. I have always been a fan of checklists for organising my life, but cleaning was not something I typically used them for until I moved in with my partner, Konan. Ah, young love! It was such an exciting time, moving in with my boyfriend and all, but I was completely unprepared for the reality of living with a man. Who knew they'd never change the toilet roll, or that they'd use up my fancy skincare products or never put things back where they belong? I felt like Monica from *Friends* when she cried, 'And now I have to live with a boy!' Whether you are moving in with a partner, a flatmate or someone else, it can be a challenge when two or more people from different walks of life come together. Everyone has a different definition of clean, and let's just say that Konan wasn't the tidiest person I'd ever met, so we had our fair share of arguments about it. But, like any normal couple, I'm sure there were things I did that drove him crazy too.

Luckily, Konan came up with a brilliant idea to create a cleaning timetable to keep our home tidy. Writing things down can be a powerful tool in unlearning bad habits. Since we were both working full-time, we divided our chores into a schedule, and it has been a lifesaver for us. I now work from home, and we still use it to this day, with some adjustments. We have a routine that works for us, and it has made our lives so much easier.

In this chapter, I want to share with you some of the schedules and checklists that I use on a daily, weekly, monthly and yearly basis, which work well for me. You can use them as a reference to create your own routine. Remember, no list is set in stone, and you should be flexible with it. If something needs to be cleaned, don't wait, and feel free to swap things around as needed. Knowing what to clean and when is half the battle when it comes to keeping your home tidy. Everyone has their unique ways of doing things, and no two households are the same. By sharing my routine and what works for me, I hope to help you create your own.

My Daily Cleaning Routine

I have a daily routine that I follow to keep my home clean and organised. I make it a habit to make my bed first thing in the morning. It sets my intentions for the day and puts me in a productive mindset to accomplish other tasks. After that, Konan takes out the rubbish before heading off to work. As I work from home, I take on the responsibility of daily cleaning tasks. Throughout the day, I make sure to wash any dirty dishes and put them away. This helps me keep the kitchen clean and tidy. I also wipe down the counters and sink after every use, and clean the stovetop after cooking. I try to do a quick sweep of the kitchen to put away any stray objects, such as loose papers or other items. If there are any spills or messes, I clean them up immediately to avoid bigger problems down the line. I also clean the bathroom sink and toilet every day to keep them fresh and hygienic. Tackling these small daily tasks helps me feel more relaxed and comfortable in my living space. It's a simple routine, but it works wonders in keeping my home clean and tidy.

DAILY CLEANING CHECKLIST

Here is an example of my daily cleaning checklist:

DAILY	M	T	W	T	F	S	S
Make the beds							
Wash the dishes							
Wipe counter / stovetop							
Take out the trash							
Vacuum / sweep floor							
Clean sink & toilet							

If you're interested in checking out some other cleaning schedules, you can find them on my website: www.tanyahomeinspo.com. I have options available that can help you stay on top of your household chores, so feel free to take a look and see if any of them would be helpful for you!

Weekly Cleaning Routine

In addition to my daily cleaning routine, there are certain tasks that I tackle on a weekly basis to keep my home in tip-top shape. To avoid spending hours at a time cleaning, I like to focus on one room each day. For example, on Mondays, I clean the kitchen, on Tuesdays, I focus on the bathroom, and so on. This way, I'm able to tackle deep-cleaning tasks without feeling overwhelmed or spending too much time on them at once. Here are some of the tasks I do every week to keep my home clean, comfortable and tidy:

- I dust all surfaces, including furniture, shelves and decorations. Then I thoroughly vacuum and mop the floors to eliminate dirt.

- I clean the mirrors and disinfect the sink, shower, bathtub and toilet in the bathroom to keep them sanitised and fresh. I also wash and change the bathmat, towels, bed sheets and pillowcases.

- In the kitchen, I wipe and disinfect all surfaces, including the stovetop, inside the microwave, and any appliances that need cleaning, such as the fridge or oven. I also get rid of any expired food, empty the bin and wipe the inside and outside of it.

- I sort through any paperwork, magazines and letters, and fluff pillows and throws.

WEEKLY CLEANING CHECKLIST

Here is an example of a weekly cleaning checklist:

MONDAY: KITCHEN

- ○ Clean microwave, toaster and kettle
- ○ Wipe down fridge
- ○ Throw out expired food
- ○ Wipe down appliances
- ○ Wipe all cabinets
- ○ Clean kitchen table

TUESDAY: BATHROOM

- ○ Deep-clean toilet
- ○ Scrub sink and bathtub
- ○ Wipe mirrors and tiles
- ○ Mop floor
- ○ Wash towels and mats
- ○ Refill toilet paper

WEDNESDAY: BEDROOM

- ○ Wipe down furniture
- ○ Dust all areas
- ○ Put away clothes
- ○ Declutter/tidy up
- ○ Wash/change bedding
- ○ Vacuum/sweep floor

THURSDAY: LIVING ROOM

- ○ Dust all areas
- ○ Vacuum/sweep floor
- ○ Wipe down furniture
- ○ Declutter/tidy up
- ○ Vacuum sofas and chairs

FRIDAY: ALL ROOMS

- ○ Wipe doors and switches
- ○ Organise mail/flyers
- ○ Clean outside the home, i.e. patio, doors, driveway, fencing, outdoor furniture
- ○ Tidy up hallway
- ○ Clean skirting boards and windows
- ○ Mop all floors

Monthly Cleaning Routine

Monthly cleaning is a great opportunity to focus on the often overlooked but frequently used areas of your home. This time gives you a chance to dig deeper into areas that might have been forgotten and have the potential to affect the lifespan of your household items. As part of your monthly cleaning routine, it's best to tackle the often-neglected areas, such as behind large appliances and furniture, which can accumulate dust and dirt over time. Additionally, take the time to deep clean your oven and refrigerator and freezer interiors. This will help keep them in top condition and prevent the build-up of harmful bacteria. Discard food in the freezer that's past its prime.

You might also clean the water tray and filter on your refrigerator, as well as the house's gutters and air vents, which can help improve the air quality inside your home. To freshen up the drains, use lemon juice, boiling water and baking soda. Additionally, wipe the interior and exterior doors, and clean telephones, light switches and windows. Furthermore, this could be the perfect time to examine your upholstered furniture for stains and clean them accordingly. By addressing these areas on a monthly basis, you can maintain a clean and healthy living space that is conducive to relaxation and productivity.

Here is an example of a monthly cleaning checklist:

MONTHLY CLEANING CHECKLIST

Monthly Tasks	J	F	M	A	M	J	J	A	S	O	N	D
Clean behind furniture												
Deep-clean oven												
Deep-clean fridge/freezer												
Discard out-of-date food in the freezer												
Clean windows												
Descale kettle												
Clean microwave												
Clean gutters and air vents												
Freshen all drains												
Wipe down all doors and light switches												
Empty and clean car												
Clean and disinfect bins												

Tasks to Complete Every Three to Six Months

Keeping a clean and organised home requires regular maintenance of various household items. While some cleaning tasks need to be done on a daily or weekly basis, others can be done every three to six months. These include vacuuming the mattress and flipping it every six months to prevent sagging and wear (see page 80). Similarly, it's important to clean and freshen the vacuum cleaner every three months to ensure maximum efficiency. Other tasks include cleaning and descaling the coffee maker, scrubbing grout (see page 54) and polishing stainless-steel appliances (see page 31). Additionally, it's important to clean and condition leather (see page 67) and wood furniture (see page 64) and wooden chopping boards (see page 43), clean blinds and curtains, and wipe down skirting boards (see page 86). By keeping up with these cleaning tasks on a regular basis, you can ensure that your home stays clean and in good working order all year round.

Here is an example of a checklist:

THREE-TO-SIX-MONTH CHECKLIST

- ◯ Clean vacuum cleaner
- ◯ Vacuum and flip mattress
- ◯ Descale the kettle
- ◯ Clean washing machine and dishwasher
- ◯ Polish stainless-steel appliances
- ◯ Clean and condition leather furniture
- ◯ Wipe down skirting boards
- ◯ Clean and condition wooden furniture and chopping boards
- ◯ Clean blinds and curtains; check for mould
- ◯ Declutter bathroom
- ◯ Clean shower hose, sinks and bath
- ◯ Wipe kitchen cabinets and fridge doors
- ◯ Vacuum sofa

Annual Cleaning Routine

Annual cleaning tasks are a great opportunity to focus on the areas of your home that require a deep clean. These tasks may feel daunting, but they only need to be done once a year. Some examples include removing the contents of kitchen cabinets and food pantries and cleaning their interiors. It's also important to throw away expired food items, deep-clean your oven and refrigerator, and clean out your wardrobe, donating or selling clothes and items you no longer use. Additionally, consider having your carpet and upholstery professionally cleaned if necessary. Finally, wiping down walls can help maintain a clean and fresh living space (see page 84).

SPRING CLEANING

Spring cleaning is an annual task that allows you to deep clean and declutter your home ahead of summer. Did you know that over 93 per cent of British households participate in cleaning activities during the spring months? People commit to a few hours a week or more of purging, cleaning and organising. It's a real thing, when people are serious about cleaning their homes. I love spring cleaning my home because it gives me a chance to tackle those neglected areas and all the mess that has accumulated in my home over the winter months.

By doing spring cleaning, you can improve your indoor air quality, reduce stress levels and create a more organised and peaceful living environment. Scan the QR code for access to my free spring-cleaning checklist.

How to Make Your Own Cleaning Schedule

If you're looking to stay organised and keep your home clean, creating your own personalised cleaning schedule can be a helpful tool. Here are some simple steps to follow:

Evaluate your cleaning needs: Take a look around your home and assess which areas require regular cleaning. This could include tasks such as vacuuming, dusting, mopping and cleaning bathrooms.

1 **Prioritise your tasks:** Determine which cleaning tasks are most important and need to be done more frequently. For example, you might want to prioritise cleaning the kitchen and bathroom over other areas.

2 **Develop a weekly schedule:** Split your cleaning tasks throughout the week, assigning specific days for each task. This approach can help you avoid overwhelming cleaning sessions and spread out the workload.

3 **Be realistic:** Set reasonable goals for yourself and avoid overloading your schedule with too many tasks in one day. It's better to create a consistent routine that you can stick to.

4 **Share responsibilities:** If you live with others, consider delegating cleaning tasks to different family members or roommates. Sharing the workload can make it more manageable and create a sense of teamwork.

5 **Stay consistent:** Try to stick to your cleaning schedule as much as possible. Consistency is key to maintaining a clean and organised home.

6 **Be flexible:** If you miss a cleaning day, adjust your schedule and make up for it later. Life can get busy, and unexpected events may arise, so it's important to be flexible and tweak your schedule as needed.

7 Remember that a cleaning schedule is intended to assist you in maintaining a clean and organised living space. Now that you have a few examples of checklists and tools on how to create your own schedules, do create your own versions. I don't believe in dictating how many hours you should spend cleaning or what should be prioritised. Rather, you should determine that for yourself. For instance, you might decide that having a clean kitchen is more important than having a clean bedroom, or that having a tidy living room is more crucial than tidying up the children's playroom. You may prefer to clean on specific days of the week rather than every day, and you shouldn't feel guilty about that. We're all individuals with unique life experiences and desires. So, please customise your cleaning routines to suit your needs and preferences, and don't forget to reward yourself for your hard work and a job well done!

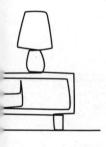

PART 2

HOME
HACKS

A few summers ago, me and my girlies - Chanelle, Shante, Pricella, Alvanis and Kandis - went to Center Parcs for the weekend and had the best time. You know what it's like: when a trip finally makes it out of the group chat, it's a big deal! We had a great holiday filled with fun, laughs and adventures. The weather was hot (which, let's be honest, is a rarity in the UK), and we enjoyed the beautiful forest, picturesque lake and tropical water park.

The true highlight of the trip, though, was the 'friendship therapy' we had. We talked about our obsession with organisation, shared tips on how to make our homes smell amazing, discussed interior design hacks and recommended some of our favourite home accounts on Instagram. We also shamelessly admitted to how disorganised our homes can be at times. We bonded over some of the struggles we face, such as keeping our homes clean while working full-time jobs. There were moments of joy and validation - therapy at its finest! That's just some of the things I love about my friends: they never judge, they always make me feel supported, and they truly understand the struggles that come with adulting.

Over the years, I have picked up various home-improvement tips from my family, friends, colleagues and even some of my followers online. In fact, once, I put out a post on Instagram asking for people's favourite helpful home hacks, and moments later my inbox was flooded with so many helpful tips - everyone understood the assignment! Now, I can pass on everything I have learnt to you.

In this section of the book, I have put together some of my favourite home hacks that I have come across over the years to help you make the best of your home. These include ways to transform your house into a beautiful, organised and comfortable haven, with decorating ideas, tips to tackle pests and hints to make your garden thrive, and also how to make your home a welcoming space when you are hosting the ones you love - whether it's a family birthday party or your very own friendship therapy session.

CHAPTER 11

HOW TO FRESHEN YOUR HOME

We all want our homes to smell clean and fresh, don't we? After all, a beautifully scented home is like a warm hug that welcomes you every time you walk in. But, let's face it, there are all kinds of odours that develop naturally in the home, such as overflowing bins, cooking smells, pet urine and smelly shoes. Your home has a unique scent that you might have become immune to, but that doesn't mean your guests are immune to it too! My biggest fear is having people over and them pinching their nose at how my home smells. It's always nice for your living space to smell clean and inviting for yourself, your family and your guests.

I have always been obsessed with nice scents, whether they be candles, reed diffusers or air fresheners. Honestly, I don't need diamonds and pearls, but if you buy me something that will make my home smell good, I'll be your best friend. One of the perks of lockdown was that I had a lot of time to experiment with new ways to keep my home smelling fresh without breaking the bank, and now I can share those tips with you.

Rice Air Freshener

You may already know that rice can be used for many things beyond eating, such as craft projects, face and hair treatments, or even to fertilise plants. But did you know that it also works as a natural odour absorber? To make a jar of scented rice, mix 10 to 20 drops of your favourite essential oils, such as rosemary, lemon or lavender oil, with 200g (¾ cup) of uncooked rice in a jar. Stir the mixture well, leaving it either open or closed with a lid that has holes. Then place it in your bathroom, closet or living room to combat unpleasant smells.

Scented Cotton Balls

Put a few drops of vanilla extract on a cotton ball and stick it in your drawer or place it under your bin liner. This will mask any odours and fill the space with a lovely scent. You can store your cotton balls in a sealed jar when not in use to preserve their scent. It's an easy and inexpensive way to improve the overall aroma of your home.

TANYA'S TIP

Try adding several drops of your favourite essential oil to a few cotton balls and then put them inside your vacuum dust bin. As you vacuum your floors, the essential oils will be released into the air, creating a subtle but refreshing scent throughout your home.

Scented Sachets

In a mixing bowl, combine 300g (1¼ cups) of Epsom salts with 10 drops of your preferred essential oil, then use a funnel to fill organza bags with the fragrant salt. These scented sachets are easy, fast and cost-effective to make, and they make great little gifts for occasions such as birthdays, Mother's Day and bridal showers. In general, the sachets stay fragrant for six months to a year. You can use them to freshen up various things. Place them in your wardrobe, your gym bag, your underwear drawer or your trainers, or hang them in your car.

Freshen Bin Odours

It's not surprising that your rubbish bin can start to smell bad over time due to the combination of food scraps and other waste. However, there is an easy way to freshen it up. You can mix 120g (½ cup) of baking soda with 10 drops of your favourite essential oil, then sprinkle the mixture into the bin when you replace the liner. Alternatively, you can layer a little bit of fragranced baking soda on top of the trash as it accumulates. This will help to eliminate the unpleasant odour and keep your home smelling fresh.

DIY Reed Diffusers

While we love a good scented candle, it needs to be manned at all times, and nobody's got time for that. However, with reed diffusers, they are long-lasting, flame-free and they look cute in your home. To make your homemade reed diffuser, pour 60ml (¼ cup) of sweet almond oil into a glass jar with a narrow opening and add your preferred essential oil(s). I personally love a fresh citrus scent – 15 drops of lemon oil and 15 drops of grapefruit oil do the trick for me. Then add 8 to 10 reed sticks (these can be bought online) to the jar and turn them over after two to three hours to help the oil travel up the sticks and fill your home with the aroma. Make sure to place the jar in a spot away from children and pets, and enjoy the lovely decorative scent!

DIY Coffee Bean Candle

Who knew that coffee beans could do more than just give us a caffeine boost in the morning? I recently discovered that they can also make our homes smell amazing! It's the newest hack that I stumbled upon while scrolling through TikTok, and I became obsessed with it faster than I can drink a latte. So, here's the deal: pour some coffee beans into a glass container or bowl and place a tealight candle in the centre of them, pushing it down slightly so that it's surrounded by the beans. Then, light the candle and let the heat fill your room with the scent of the coffee beans. You can choose between plain coffee beans or give hazelnut or French vanilla a try for a scrumptious smell that will make your whole house smell like a cappuccino. Give it a try – you'll thank me later!

Hang Eucalyptus in Your Shower

If you're looking for an easy and affordable way to make your bathroom smell amazing, consider tying eucalyptus leaves around your shower head. This simple DIY trick is a natural and effective way to create a spa-like atmosphere while you shower. To create your eucalyptus shower bundle, simply gather a handful of fresh eucalyptus leaves and tie them together with a piece of twine or ribbon. Then hang the bundle from your shower head so that the leaves are positioned in the path of the water. As you shower, the steam and heat will activate the natural oils in the eucalyptus leaves, releasing a refreshing and invigorating aroma that can help clear your sinuses and lift your mood. Plus, eucalyptus is known for its antibacterial and antifungal properties, which can help to keep your shower clean, fresh and smelling amazing. Not only is this DIY hack easy and affordable, but it's also a stylish and natural way to add a touch of greenery to your bathroom decor.

Laundry Scent Boosters

Try filling organza bags with laundry scent boosters, such as Lenor (UK) or Downy beads (US). Put the bags inside your cushion covers, and your sofa and living room will smell incredible. Alternatively, you can also use tumble-dryer sheets in the same way.

DIY Room and Linen Spray

Making your own air freshener from scratch may sound tricky, but it's actually a simple process – trust me! I often get messages about the best way to freshen your home without the use of harsh chemicals. I understand why people might be hesitant about using commercial air fresheners due to the chemicals they contain. Some store-bought air fresheners can be overly perfumed, which can even cause headaches. Between body perfumes and toxic air fresheners, we are circulating more and more chemicals in the air. But there's no need to worry – by making your own room spray at home, you can ensure that your home smells great without using any harmful chemicals. All you need are a few inexpensive ingredients and a few spare minutes.

Mix 180ml (¾ cup) of distilled water (or cooled boiled water) with 25 drops of the essential oils of your choice and 2 tablespoons of alcohol (vodka or rubbing alcohol – see page 28). Vodka is helpful in dispersing the essential oils in the room spray, as oil and water don't mix. However, if you prefer an alcohol-free recipe, you can simply use essential oils and water. Funnel the mixture into a 250ml spray bottle and seal tightly. The essential oils tend to sit on top of the water, so always shake well before spraying.

You can use this homemade room and linen spray whenever you need a quick blast of freshness, or on a daily basis to fill your room with a hint of fragrance. I spray mine on my furniture, bedding and carpets to freshen up my home. Keep in mind that natural homemade air fresheners may not last as long as commercial chemical air fresheners. As a result, you may need to spray them more frequently. However, I personally don't mind this since they are much safer and healthier for you and your loved ones.

Simmer Pots

Simmer pots, also known as stovetop potpourri, are a simple and inexpensive way to make your home smell amazing without the use of harsh chemicals. To make a simmer pot, fill a saucepan with 500ml (2 cups) of water and add your favourite spices, herbs and fruit, such as sliced oranges, apples, cinnamon sticks, ginger, cloves, cranberries, rosemary, vanilla and more. Bring the ingredients to the boil, then reduce the heat and let the mixture simmer to fill your home with a beautiful aroma. Keep an eye on it and add water as needed. You can add leftover scraps like orange and lemon peels or apple skins to your simmer pot, making it an environmentally friendly and natural way to scent your home. It's a great habit to have a simmer pot on a few times a week after cooking. You can get creative with the ingredients and have fun with it. Win!

TANYA'S TIP

To make a simmer pot in a slow cooker, add the water and your ingredients, then cover with the lid. Turn the slow cooker to high until steam starts to roll off the lid. Once that happens, remove the lid and reduce the slow cooker to a low setting. Make sure to add water as needed to keep it at least halfway full. Your home will smell amazeballs!

SIMMER POT RECIPES TO GET YOU STARTED

Cinnamon Orange Simmer Pot

500ml (2 cups) water, peel of 1 orange (or 1 sliced orange), 3 cinnamon sticks, 1 teaspoon of cloves, 1 teaspoon of vanilla extract

Pumpkin Spice

500ml (2 cups) water, 1 sliced apple, 1 teaspoon of pumpkin spice seasoning, 2 cinnamon sticks, 1 teaspoon of ground nutmeg, a drop of vanilla extract

Cinnamon Apple Simmer Pot

500ml (2 cups) water, 2 cinnamon sticks, 2 sliced apples, 1 sliced orange, 1 teaspoon of cloves

Lemon and Rosemary Simmer Pot

500ml (2 cups) water, 3 sprigs of rosemary, 1 sliced lemon, 1 teaspoon of vanilla extract, 1 teaspoon of black peppercorns

Christmas Simmer Pot

500ml (2 cups) water, 1 sliced orange, 1 sliced apple, 2 cinnamon sticks, 1 teaspoon of cloves, 25g (½ cup) pine needles, 250g (1 cup) cranberries

Autumn Simmer Pot

500ml (2 cups) water, 1 sliced apple, 1 sliced lemon, 1 sliced orange, 2 bay leaves, 2 cinnamon sticks, 2 sprigs of rosemary, 1 teaspoon of vanilla extract

Spring Simmer Pot

500ml (2 cups) water, 1 sliced lime, a handful of mint, 2 bay leaves, 4 sprigs of thyme, 1 teaspoon of vanilla extract

Lavender Simmer Pot

500ml (2 cups) water, peel of 1 lemon (or 1 sliced lemon), 6 sprigs of dried or fresh lavender, 2 sprigs of rosemary

CHAPTER 12

HOME
IMPROVEMENTS

Starting a home renovation project can be overwhelming. Even after spending hours on Pinterest and watching multiple YouTube videos for inspiration, it can be hard to know where to begin. Renovating can also be more expensive than you anticipated. However, you don't need to get into debt to renovate, decorate or refresh a room. Sometimes small changes can make a big difference, and having the right tools will help you complete tasks more efficiently.

When my partner, Konan, and I first started decorating our home, we faced a few challenges. For one, we had a limited budget, so we had to get creative with our decor choices. I scoured charity shops for unique pieces that I could repurpose or refurbish to fit our vision. Additionally, we had to consider the size of our home, and how the layout would affect the flow and functionality of the space. But despite these challenges, we were determined to create a beautiful and inviting space that we could be proud of. We worked together to come up with a design plan that incorporated our individual tastes and preferences. We compromised on certain aspects and made sacrifices where necessary, but ultimately, we were able to create a space that reflected both of our personalities and styles.

Throughout the process, we learnt the importance of patience, perseverance and teamwork. We faced setbacks and obstacles along the way, but we didn't let them discourage us. Instead, we kept our eyes on the end goal and remained committed to seeing the project through to completion. Now, whenever we walk into our home, we feel a sense of pride and accomplishment. We overcame the challenges that stood in our way and created a space that we love and enjoy spending time in. So, here, I have put together some tips and tricks that will have you tackling that next home-improvement project with confidence and have your home looking Pinterest-worthy in no time. We hope that our experience can serve as inspiration for others who are looking to transform their own living spaces on a budget.

Spruce Up Your Home with a Quick Lick of Paint

Give your home a lift with a fresh touch of paint. A simple coat of paint can completely transform a room, bringing new life and energy to the space. Whether you're looking to brighten up a dull room or add a pop of colour to a neutral space, painting is a quick, easy and affordable way to make a big impact. Plus, with so many colours and finishes to choose from, you can easily find a shade that fits your style and personality. So why not take the plunge and give your home a mini-makeover with a new paint colour? It's a small change that can make a big difference.

TANYA'S TIP

Once you are finished with painting for the day, wrap the roller or paintbrush in aluminium foil, then put it in a plastic bag, and then (here's the secret) put it in the fridge. This trick will keep the roller or brush fresh between coats until you're ready to paint again, with no need to wash it! Please note, however, that this trick only works if you plan to continue painting the next day or the day after. The roller or brush can only be stored for a maximum of two days.

Use Painter's Tape

To achieve clean and sharp paint lines, as well as to protect your surfaces from unwanted drips and splatters, it's recommended that you use painter's tape along the edges of the walls and ceilings, around fixtures, and on trims and moulding. This is also a smart way to keep sealant between the lines when you're redoing it around your bathtub or shower.

The Easy Way to Remove Wallpaper

Removing old wallpaper can be a time-consuming and tedious task, but using the right tools can speed up the process. You don't need to buy a professional scorer, as a fork can do the job just as well. Run the fork over the wallpaper's surface, which will lift pieces of wallpaper from the wall and allow steam or solution to penetrate freely. Renting a steamer is recommended to loosen the glue and lift the wallpaper seamlessly, but in case the steamer doesn't work well, mix equal parts of white vinegar and warm water in a spray bottle. Spritz the solution generously over the wallpapered area. Once soaked, the paper should come off the walls easily.

Paint Your Grout

Grout-reviver pens are the perfect little tools for restoring and refreshing old grouting that has become faded and discoloured. To refresh your bathroom or kitchen tile grout, simply use the pen to paint over the grout lines and let it set (wipe away any excess on the tiles with a sponge or cloth using warm water) usually for 60 minutes, or according to the instructions – and you'll have bright, clean grout lines again.

Update Your Kitchen Hardware

Upgrading your cabinet hardware is an easy kitchen update that can make a huge difference. If you don't have enough money for a full-scale kitchen renovation, you'll be surprised at how much of an impact it can have. Installing new knobs or handles can make your cupboards and drawers look spick and span. It is a quick process that can be done in just a few hours but has the ability to transform the entire appearance and feel of the space.

Install a New Ceiling Light in Your Entry Way

The entryway is the first impression visitors get of your house, so it's important to make it look appealing and up-to-date. Installing a new ceiling light is a great way to transform a space from blah to beautiful! There are many options, ranging from chandeliers to flush lights and pendant lights. Choosing a new style that fits with the rest of your home is a great way to go. Additionally, it's important to choose a light fixture that is to scale with the size of the room and provides enough light. However, keep in mind that electrical work can be dangerous, so it's always better to call in a professional to do the wiring if you're unsure.

Try a Peel-and-stick Splashback

If your kitchen or bathroom needs a refresh, you could consider purchasing self-adhesive splashback tiles to transform your existing ones. These peel-and-stick tiles are perfect if you want to install a new backsplash but don't want to undertake a huge, expensive project. They are versatile and allow you to easily add some colour and texture to your home. This is a quick, budget-friendly makeover that is easy to do and a perfect solution for creating a trendy look in your home for a fraction of the price.

Update Countertops Using Vinyl Wrap

When we decided to update our kitchen, one of the first things we tackled was the countertops. Due to our limited budget, we couldn't afford to replace them, so we chose to use d-c-fix, a self-adhesive vinyl wrap, instead, which can cover a variety of surfaces in the home. The results were amazing, and our kitchen looked so much better. It's a perfect solution for those looking to transform their countertops on a budget. Plus, it's an excellent option for renters, since it's easily removable. The vinyl wrap comes in a variety of colours and patterns, making it easy to find a design that fits your personal style, and installing it is a simple process that can be done in just a few hours. So whether you're looking to update your kitchen, bathroom or any other space in your home, vinyl wrap is an excellent option for those on a budget.

Swap Out Old Taps

If you are unable to afford a complete kitchen or bathroom renovation, small upgrades can make a big difference. Consider replacing old taps and faucets, particularly if they are over ten years old. This will not only enhance the appearance of your space, but also conserve water, since newer faucets are more environmentally friendly.

Hide Unsightly Wires

You can easily hide unsightly wires using cable covers. We use them at home to hide our annoying TV cables, which hang down and ruin our aesthetic. They are easy to install with a peel-and-stick application and they blend with the wall perfectly. Another way to hide wires is by placing them in a decorative basket. A simple woven or fabric basket can do wonders to organise all those unattractive wires pooling around your TV, computer and other electronics. Another option is to drill or cut a medium-sized hole into the back panel of your storage units. This will give you space to feed the cords through, allowing you to discreetly plug in your devices.

Make Curtains Look Custom

Being budget-conscious does not mean you have to sacrifice on style. If you want to elevate your living space but don't want to spend a lot of money, consider giving your curtains a custom look. You can make inexpensive curtains look custom-made by using a few simple tricks. First, choose the right fabric. Look for heavy, high-quality fabrics such as linen or velvet that hang well and give the illusion of expensive drapes. Next, add some embellishments, like tassels, fringe or ribbon, to the edges of the curtains. This will give them

a more polished look. Finally, hang your curtains high and wide to make your windows appear larger and create a more dramatic effect. With these tips, you can easily transform your inexpensive curtains into custom drapes.

Use Mirrors to Make a Room Look Bigger

Not only do mirrors make your home look beautiful, but they can also be used to create the illusion of a larger room. If placed strategically, they can reflect light and give the impression of more space. For example, a large mirror hung on the wall opposite a window can reflect natural light and make the room feel brighter and more open. Mirrors can also be used to create depth in a room by placing them at an angle or in a group. Additionally, they can be used to reflect decorative items in the room, creating the illusion of more furniture or accessories. It's a simple and affordable way to enhance the look of your home while also making it feel more open and welcoming. Plus, mirrors come in all shapes and sizes, so you can find the perfect one to fit your decor style.

Refresh Your Space with an Area Rug

Adding an area rug to your room is a simple and effective way to bring a pop of colour and a fresh feel to your space. Even if you have wall-to-wall carpeting, an area rug can help redirect attention if your carpet has seen better days or if you have messy kids or pets. The best part is that area rugs come in a variety of sizes, shapes and designs, making it easy to find one that fits your style and budget.

To choose the right rug for your room, start by considering the size and shape of the rug in relation to the room's dimensions and furniture layout. Next, choose a colour or pattern that complements the existing decor or adds a dash of colour to the room. When placing the rug, make sure it's centred and level. If you have hardwood or tile floors, use a rug pad to prevent slipping and sliding. Finally, consider layering different sizes and textures of rugs for a unique and cosy look.

Art Will Add Personality to Your Home

Darlings, let's talk about art, shall we? Because let's face it, your home is more than just a place to crash after a long day; it's a reflection of your fabulous personality. That's where art comes in! It's like a magic wand that can transform any room into a warm and inviting sanctuary that screams YOU. Whether it's a captivating landscape, a thought-provoking abstract piece or even a family portrait, each art selection has the power to add character and charm to your living space. There are endless affordable options to choose from. And if you're feeling adventurous, why not switch up your prints or even create your own masterpiece? The options are endless, just like your creativity!

Plant Power

Bringing the outdoors in is one of my favourite ways to decorate my home. Plants have the power to transform any space. They add colour, texture and life to a room, creating a natural and peaceful atmosphere. Plants can be used to fill empty corners, brighten up a dull room and add a touch of nature to your living space. Moreover, they are known for their air-purifying properties so can improve the air quality of your home. Whether you choose to display them on a windowsill, hang them from the ceiling or place them on a shelf, plants can instantly transform the feel of your space. They also come in a variety of shapes, sizes and colours, making it easy to find ones that fit your style. So, if you're looking to spruce up your home and create a welcoming atmosphere, consider adding some greenery to your space.

Below is a list of some of my favourite houseplants:

— **Monstera:** Also known as the Swiss cheese plant, Monstera a tropical plant with large, fenestrated leaves that can grow to be quite large. The Monstera is an excellent statement piece for any room and adds a touch of drama and tropical vibes to your space.

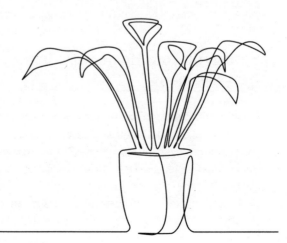

- **Bird of paradise:** Another stunning tropical plant with large, paddle-shaped leaves that can grow striking orange and blue flowers that resemble a bird in flight. They make a bold statement and add a pop of colour to your space.

- **Golden pothos:** This is a hanging plant known for its vining growth habit and heart-shaped leaves. It's easy to care for and can grow in a variety of lighting conditions, making it a great choice for beginners. Plus, its trailing vines can add a touch of greenery and texture to any room.

- **Aloe vera:** A succulent known for its medicinal properties and its ability to thrive with minimal care. It's a great addition to any room and can help to improve the air quality in your home.

Some people find it challenging to keep plants alive and thriving, especially if you have a busy lifestyle or are unable to dedicate time to plant care. In this case, artificial plants can be a great alternative to real plants. They come in a variety of sizes, shapes and styles, and can look just as realistic as real plants. They are a cost-effective option for having greenery in your home and can add a touch of beauty and life to your living space.

Spruce Up Your Home with Some New Cushions

Do you ever get bored of the same room set-up after a few months? I know I do! But that doesn't mean I have to buy new furniture every season; that would be too expensive and impractical. Instead, I like to switch things up by adding new cushions to my sofa or bed. Introducing different colours and textures into your home makes it visually appealing. Regardless of whether you live in a small flat or a mansion, decorative cushions are versatile accessories that can give your home a unique touch. With their varied colours, textures and patterns, they can make your sofa or bed a conversation starter.

Enhance Your Home with Candles

Candles are my obsession, and my house is proof of it. I have them in every nook and cranny, but I'm still not done! Candles are perfect for adding elegance, warmth and cosiness to any home. They come in all shapes, sizes and colours, making them perfect for any space. You can choose from pillar, votive or taper candles, depending on your mood and the occasion. And, if you're feeling fancy, you can pair them with candle holders, lanterns or decorative trays to create a stunning centrepiece. The possibilities with candles are endless, just like my love for them! They also come in a wide range of scents, which can help mask any unpleasant odours in your home and create a more pleasant and inviting atmosphere. You can choose from floral, fruity or even woody scents to suit your preference. I love going around the shops and sniffing all the different scents available; there's something for everyone.

TANYA'S TIP

Are you tired of your candles not melting evenly? You can prevent this issue, called candle tunnelling, with a quick and easy hack. The problem usually happens when you don't let a new candle burn long enough during its first use, but what can you do if your candle just won't melt all the way around? Simply wrap a piece of aluminium foil around the top of the candle, making sure the wick has enough room to burn safely. Fold the foil slightly around the inner part where the wick is, being careful to keep it clear of the flame. In a few hours, the wax around the sides will melt down, and the candle will burn evenly.

Rearrange the Room

Here's a cost-free idea for revamping a room that requires only your physical effort and motivation. Have you noticed how simply shifting your existing furniture around and restyling your shelves can give your room an exhilarating new feel? By simply changing the position of your furniture or adding a few decorative pieces, you can transform the look and atmosphere of your space – and it's fun too. Start by thinking about the function of your room and how you want it to feel. Consider factors such as lighting, colour and texture to create a cohesive design. You can also experiment with different layouts until you find the one that works best for your needs. Rearranging a room can breathe new life into your home and make it feel like a completely different space.

CHAPTER 13

HOSTING

There are two types of people in this world: those who can't stand hosting, and those who live for it. Me? I fall into the latter category – let me tell you why.

Back in my university days, my housemates and I threw our first party. We invited a few people, who invited a few more, and before we knew it crowds of people were packed into our house like sardines in a can. It was so crammed you had to literally walk sideways just to make it to the bathroom. But, man, was it a good time. The drinks were flowing, the music was popping and everyone was having a blast. Some of my housemates were a bit overwhelmed by the number of people, but not me. Being an extrovert, I was in my element!

For me, hosting is more than just a hobby or a way to pass the time. It is a true passion that brings me immense joy and fulfilment. There's just something magical about welcoming people into your home, sharing food, drinks and stories, and creating memories that will last a lifetime. Today, I love nothing more than sharing my home with friends, family and loved ones. Whether it's a small and intimate gathering or a big, festive party, I strive to make my guests feel comfortable, happy and cared for.

Over the years, I've learnt a lot about hosting, from the art of decorating to the science of cooking, from the importance of planning to the joy of seeing my guests having a great time. In this chapter, I want to share my top tips on how to make your next gathering a memorable and enjoyable one. You might be hosting a dinner party, a games night or a family brunch;

whatever it is, these hacks will help you create an atmosphere that is warm and welcoming. You'll learn how to set the right ambience, curate the perfect menu and create a comfortable seating arrangement, so you can become a confident and gracious host. So let's get started and explore the wonderful world of hosting together!

Host on a Budget

One of the biggest misconceptions about hosting an event is that you need to spend a lot of money to make it memorable. However, this is far from the truth. With a little creativity, you can create a fantastic atmosphere for your guests without breaking the bank. Why not consider hosting your event at home instead of renting a venue? This can save you a lot of money on rental fees and catering costs. You could even borrow items such as tables, chairs or linens from friends or family. There are plenty of resources available online, where you can find helpful tips and tricks from experienced hosts who know how to make an impact on a shoestring. So, don't let a limited budget hold you back from throwing an unforgettable event. With a little planning and some clever ideas, you can create a memorable experience for your guests without spending a fortune

Plan Ahead

Planning is the key to organising a successful event. Before you start shopping for decorations or food, make a list of everything you need and have a clear idea of what you want to source. It's important to stick to a budget and avoid making impulse buys. This will prevent you from overspending on unnecessary items and ensure that you have all the things you need to make your event a success. Additionally, consider buying in bulk to save money.

Here is a template checklist that you can use to begin your hosting process:

HOSTING CHECKLIST

DATE .... TIME ....

LOCATION ....

GUEST LIST

	Yes	RSVP Maybe	No
TANYA	☑	○	○
	○	○	○
	○	○	○
	○	○	○
	○	○	○
	○	○	○
	○	○	○
	○	○	○
	○	○	○
	○	○	○
	○	○	○
	○	○	○
	○	○	○
	○	○	○
	○	○	○
	○	○	○
	○	○	○
	○	○	○
	○	○	○

THEMES/DECORATIONS

FOOD & DRINKS

ENTERTAINMENT

Keep Your Guestlist Short

While your typical party mantra may be 'the more, the merrier', when you're hosting an event, you need to consider keeping it more intimate whenever possible as it can significantly reduce the cost. With a shorter guest list, you'll need to buy and prepare less food and drink, and fewer goody bags if you're giving them, and might not have to purchase additional plates or other essentials for the event.

Invite Your Guests

Don't forget to invite your guests to your event – trust me, it happens! You can create a Facebook event or send out a group text message to let everyone know the date, time and location. You could share the itinerary or mention the movie, the menu and any other details, such as a dress code or parking instructions. Don't forget to ask your guests to RSVP, so you can prepare enough snacks and seating.

Ask for Help

Listen, I love cooking just as much as the next foodie, but when it comes to throwing a party for more than 30 people, I need all the help I can get! I'm not too proud to ask for helpers, or to accept if someone offers to lend a hand. My go-to response? 'Sure, bring games/desserts/drinks!' This way, I can focus on cooking up a storm without breaking the bank or losing my mind. After all, there's nothing more stressful than trying to feed a large crowd on your own. So, take it from me, whether you need extra alcohol or food, don't be afraid to ask for help – your taste buds (and your sanity) will thank you!

Speaking of help, try hosting a pot-luck-themed event! The idea of a pot-luck party is that you ask everyone to bring one dish and you have a feast. It's a sure way to save the pennies while trying varied dishes! Ensure the dishes are within your guests' budgets and cooking abilities. It is important to be clear with your instructions and to delegate where necessary. For example, if you are going for a specific theme, make sure everyone gets the memo. I usually create a shared link or WhatsApp group to track what everyone is bringing. Make sure you plan ahead too, or you may just end up with 10 dishes of macaroni cheese!

Work with What You've Got

You don't need to have fancy home decorations, expensive china plates or luxury cutlery to impress your guests. If you're hosting at home, chances are that your space is already cosy and inviting. Added extras are not necessary and may not even make a good impression on your guests. Use what you already have at home, such as serving dishes, glassware and tablecloths. Remember, hosting on a budget doesn't have to mean sacrificing quality or style.

DIY Decorations

Before you decide to buy decorations, ask yourself whether you could make them yourself. This can be a great way to add a personal touch to your party while also saving money. It's a fun and creative activity that can involve your friends or family, and the end result can be truly unique and special. You can buy art and craft supplies in bulk, which can be used for future events or repurposed for other projects. Attention to detail is key, and even the smallest touches can elevate your decor.

With a little creativity, you can make beautiful and memorable decorations that will impress your guests without breaking the bank.

There are numerous DIY decoration ideas that you can utilise to make your next party more fun and colourful:

- Create a banner using coloured paper, glue and string. Cut out different shapes, such as triangles or circles, from the paper, and glue them onto the string.

- Set up a photo booth by hanging up colourful fabric or patterned paper as a backdrop and adding some fun props like hats, glasses and moustaches.

- For a dinner party, you can create your own centrepieces using flowers, glass jars and ribbon. Simply arrange fresh flowers in the jar and tie a ribbon around the top for a charming and rustic look.

- For an alternative centrepiece idea, you can make a candle arrangement using pillar candles and decorative stones or beads.

- When I plan a movie night, I enjoy setting up a snack bar. I arrange various snacks and treats in colourful containers on a table and add some simple decorations like a movie poster or a string of fairy lights.

With these ideas as your starting point, you'll be able to create a personalised and memorable atmosphere. The options are endless when it comes to DIY decorations, so don't be afraid to get creative and make your party unique.

Host Like a Pro

To master the art of hosting, you've got to think about everything, from the theme to the timing, down to the nitty-

gritty details. What's on the menu? What's the entertainment? Where are people going to sit? It's a lot to handle, but with some practice (and maybe a few cocktails), you can become a stellar host in no time, and throw a fabulous, stress-free gathering that everyone will enjoy. Allow me to show you how.

AMBIENCE

Creating the perfect atmosphere is crucial to ensure that your guests feel at ease, engaged and ready to have a good time. Here are some tips on how to do it:

- **Lighting:** One of the most effective ways to achieve the right atmosphere is by paying careful attention to the lighting. Consider using string lights, lanterns or candles to add a touch of ambience. By using soft, warm hues, you can create a cosy and intimate setting that encourages your guests to relax and unwind. On the other hand, bright, cool lighting can be invigorating and energising, perfect for events that require a livelier vibe.

- **Music:** Music is a crucial factor in setting the tone of your event. Whether you opt for a live band or curate a playlist, the music should be carefully selected to complement the mood you want to create. Soft, calming melodies can be perfect for a spa night, while lively, upbeat tunes are ideal for a birthday party or wedding reception.

- **Smell:** Fragrance can add an extra layer to the ambience of your event. The scent of fresh flowers, aromatic candles or delicious food can enhance your guests' experience and create a welcoming, comfortable environment (see Chapter 11, How to Freshen Your Home).

DECORATIONS

When it comes to decorating for a party or gathering, there are endless possibilities, depending on your personal style and the occasion. Here are some decoration tips and ideas to help you get started:

–   **Pick a decor theme:** When it comes to decorating, picking a theme can help tie everything together and create a cohesive and memorable atmosphere. A theme can be as simple as a colour scheme or as elaborate as a specific time period or cultural celebration. Use your chosen theme as a guide for your decorations, and try making your own if your budget is tight (see page 147). Alternatively, pick a theme that you already have suitable decorations for! It's time to dust off the ol' box in the attic and see what treasures you can upcycle.

–   **Decorate the table:** A beautifully laid table can create an instant impact. A tablecloth, placemats and coordinating napkins can make all the difference. Add some candlesticks or a floral centrepiece to create a warm and inviting atmosphere.

–   **Balloons and banners:** Balloons are a fun and affordable way to add some colour and excitement to your space. Consider using them in coordinating colours or shapes to match your party's theme. Hanging banners or bunting can also add a festive touch to any space. Try using them to create a photo backdrop or to highlight a specific area of your home.

MAKE IT MEMORABLE

Hosting is not only about serving food and drinks, but also creating a memorable experience for your guests. To achieve this, you can personalise the experience to cater to your guests' interests and personalities, or add unique details that will make the occasion stand out. There are various ways to make an event unforgettable, depending on the type of gathering and the guests who will be attending. Here are some tips to help you:

- **Personal touches:** It's all about adding those little touches that make your guests feel extra special and showing them how much you appreciate them attending your event. Personalised goody bags, a custom cocktail menu and decorated place cards are just a few ways to make them feel welcomed and appreciated. I like to use my Cricut machine to create labelled cups for my guests to prevent drink mix-ups. And to really make the night memorable, consider sending your guests home with a little something to commemorate the evening. And no, I'm not talking about a hangover! (Although that is a possibility.) Why not give them a budget-friendly keepsake that they can take home? Trust me, they'll appreciate it. My go-to idea? A photo using an instant camera! Not only will it capture all the crazy moments throughout the night, but your guests will have a hilarious reminder of how much fun they had.

- **Entertainment:** To make your event more engaging and enjoyable, curate a selection of entertainment that aligns with the vibe you want to create. You can set up interactive game stations that allow your guests to engage with each other and have fun (see page 156). Games have always been real crowd-pleasers! Another great way to keep the energy high is by having some form of music or photo booth. Whether it's a curated playlist that fits with the theme of your party or a small photo booth with fun props that tie back to the event, these little touches can really elevate the experience for your guests.

– **Pick a theme:** When hosting events, choosing a theme can add a fun and unique element to the occasion. For a night with your besties, you could throw a 'Galentine's' party to celebrate your friendship. Decorate with pink and red streamers, balloons and heart-shaped confetti to create a festive atmosphere. You can also incorporate fun activities, such as making your own Valentine's Day cards or having a wine and chocolate tasting. Or, if you're in the mood for a thrill, go for a murder-mystery theme. Dress up as characters and solve a fictional crime together. A taco night can also be a fun and delicious option if you want a more relaxed atmosphere. Set up a taco bar with all the trimmings and let your guests create their own perfect mouthfuls. For a blast from the past, a Nineties party theme can be a fun way to relive the nostalgia of the decade. Encourage guests to dress up in their favourite Nineties attire, and decorate with neon colours, cassette tapes and other vintage items. You can also incorporate Nineties movies or music to help you party like it's 1999! With so many themes to choose from, the possibilities are endless. Let your imagination run wild and have a blast!

– **Make it unique:** To make your event truly special, consider incorporating something unique or unexpected. Choose an idea or activity that is fun and engaging, and let it guide your choices for everything from the decorations to the food and drinks. You can even include surprises throughout the event, such as an unexpected performance or a special guest appearance, to really keep your guests on their toes. With a little creativity and planning, you can create an event that your guests will never forget.

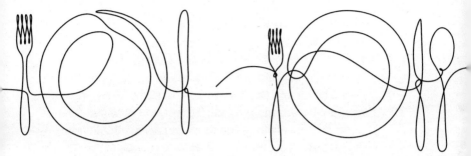

Hosting Different Types of Events

DINNER PARTY

Hosting a dinner party can be a fun and rewarding experience, but it can also be a bit overwhelming if you're not sure where to start. Whether you're planning a dinner for friends, family or co-workers, there are a few key steps you can take to ensure that your event is a success. Here are some tips and tricks that your dinner-party guests will love:

- **Plan your menu:** The first step in hosting a successful dinner party is to plan your menu. Start by considering your guests' dietary restrictions and preferences, and choose dishes that will appeal to a wide range of tastes. It's also a good idea to choose dishes that can be prepared in advance so that you're not stuck in the kitchen all night. If you're not confident in your cooking skills, consider hiring a caterer or ordering food from a local restaurant. See the next page for an example party planner to help you get started.

- **Set the table:** The presentation of your dinner table can make a huge impact on your guests' dining experience. You should choose a tablecloth or placemats that complement your dinnerware and add some candles or fresh flowers for a touch of elegance. You could even get creative and make your own table centrepieces using flowers, branches or paper cut-outs (see page

141). Folding napkins in unique ways can add a fun touch to the table setting – you can find tutorials on how to do this easily on my social-media platforms. A table runner is also an affordable way to upgrade your dining table. Don't forget to ensure that there are enough place settings for each guest, and consider using place cards to assign seats. By paying attention to these small details, you can elevate your dinner party to the next level and impress your guests.

—   **Serve a range of food and drinks:** Before dinner, you can serve your guests drinks and canapés to whet their appetites. Choose a selection of light, easy-to-eat finger foods that can be served on a platter or passed around. Offer a range of drinks, including wine, beer and non-alcoholic options. When it's time for dinner, serve the main course in a timely and organised manner. If you're hosting a sit-down dinner, consider having a designated server to help you plate up and serve the food. If you're hosting a buffet-style meal, make sure the dishes are clearly labelled and that there is enough food for everyone. If you're feeling up to it, consider serving a dessert to cap off the meal.

TANYA'S TIP

One useful hack for keeping food and drinks cold at a party is the frozen aluminium tray method. To do this, pour water into an aluminium serving tray until it's about two-thirds full, then freeze it. Once it's frozen, place another tray on top of it, and the frozen tray underneath will act as a cooler to keep your drinks and food cold as your guests arrive.

DINNER PARTY PLANNER

GUESTS
(6-8 including you)

Theme
_____
_____
_____
_____

Dietary Restirctions
_____
_____
_____

GROCERIES
_____
_____
_____
_____
_____
_____
_____
_____
_____
_____
_____
_____
_____
_____
_____
_____
_____
_____
_____
_____
_____
_____
_____
_____
_____

MENU

Arrival Cocktail/Wine
_____

Appetizer #1
_____

Appetizer #2
_____

Salad/Soup/Bread
_____
_____

Main Course Wine
_____
_____

Main Course
_____
_____

Side Dish
_____

Dessert
_____

After Dinner Drinks
_____
_____

GAMES NIGHT

Hosting games nights is one of my favourite pastimes. I enjoy bringing my friends together for a fun-filled evening of board games, card games and party games. It's always a fun time, and I get to brag about my wins after an epic showdown. It's a great way to socialise, unwind and have some laughs. Plus, it's a budget-friendly way to have a good time. Whether it's a small gathering or a big party, I always look forward to hosting games nights and creating unforgettable memories with my loved ones. Here are some tips on how to host a successful games night:

—   **Choose the right games:** This is the first step in hosting a great games night. You want games that are fun, easy to learn and can be played by a group of people. Some popular games that are perfect for games nights include Monopoly, Scrabble, charades, or truth or dare.

—   **Get the space right:** Make sure the space where you're hosting the games night is comfortable for everyone, with enough seating, and good lighting so that all your guests can see the game board or cards. You might also want to consider having some snacks and drinks available to keep everyone fuelled up and ready to play. Consider playing some background music to set the tone.

- **Keep the games moving:** One of the most important things to keep in mind when hosting a games night is to keep the games moving. Make sure everyone knows the rules and how to play so that everyone has a chance to get involved. If a game is taking too long or is boring, don't be afraid to switch it up and try something else.

- **Have fun:** Finally, remember that the whole point of hosting a games night is to have fun! Don't take things too seriously, and don't worry too much about who wins or loses. The most important thing is to spend time with your friends and family and create some great memories together.

MOVIE NIGHT

When the weather outside is cold and miserable, there's no better way to spend an evening than by inviting your friends and family over for a cosy movie night. With some delicious snacks, comfy seating and a great selection of films, you can create a warm and inviting atmosphere that everyone will enjoy. Whether you prefer classic movies or the latest Hollywood film, a home-cinema experience is a great way to relax, unwind and spend quality time with your loved ones. Here are some tips on how to host a movie night indoors:

- **Choose the right movie:** Consider the genre, the age group of your guests and the length of the movie before you decide what to watch. If you're hosting kids, choose a family-friendly movie that everyone can enjoy. If it's a group of adults, consider a classic movie or a popular comedy. You can also let your guests vote on their favourite movie beforehand to ensure that everyone is happy with the selection.

- **Create a home cinema:** Make sure the space where you're hosting the movie night is comfortable for everyone. Arrange some pillows, bean bags or blankets to create a cosy atmosphere. Dim the lights and close the curtains to create a movie-theatre environment. You can also consider adding some decorations such as movie posters or fairy lights to enhance the ambience. Additionally, create your own movie tickets to make the event feel more authentic.

— **Prepare some snacks:** Snacks are an essential part of any movie night. You don't have to spend a fortune, though. Pop some popcorn on the stove or in a popcorn maker and serve it in cute paper bags or bowls. You can even have a designated popcorn and pick-'n'-mix station and get really creative with it. Or try making some homemade snacks, such as nachos, pizza bites or cookies. If you're on a tight budget, ask your guests to bring their favourite snacks or drinks.

— **Use a streaming service:** Instead of renting or buying a DVD, use a streaming service to watch the movie. Most offer a free trial period, so you can sign up for a month and cancel it after the movie night. Alternatively, you could borrow a movie from a friend or the library if you don't have access to a streaming service.

Ideas for Date Night at Home

Date nights can be expensive and difficult to arrange when you have kids and need to find a babysitter. But who says you need to leave the house to have a romantic and memorable evening? Staying in for date night doesn't have to be boring. In fact, it can be a great opportunity to get creative and spend quality time together. Here are some tips for curating a special and intimate evening:

- **Cook a special meal:** Cooking together can be a fun bonding activity. You can choose a recipe that you both enjoy or try something new. You could even make it a competition to see who can prepare the best dish. Don't forget to set the table with your best dishes and glasses, and make it a romantic evening with some candles. You can easily create a candlelit dinner at home on a budget.

- **Have a cosy movie night:** Choose a movie that you both enjoy or take turns picking a new movie to watch. Create a cosy atmosphere with some blankets and pillows, pop some popcorn, and cuddle up on the couch to watch your favourite movie together.

- **Set up a games night for two:** Dust off your board games or card games and spend the evening playing together. Choose games that you both enjoy or try something new. You can even make it interesting by adding some friendly wagers to the games.

- **Have a picnic:** How about a picnic-style dinner at home? Spread out a blanket and relax. You could even make it more interesting by having a themed dinner – a wine and cheese night, for example. Choose a few different types of wine and cheese to try, and spend the evening tasting and discussing your favourites.

–   **Have a spa night:** Get into your bathrobes and give each other massages or facials. Create a romantic atmosphere by dimming the lights and lighting some scented candles. You might also want to play some soft, relaxing music to set the mood.

–   **Do a fun activity:** If you want to get creative, consider doing a DIY project or art activity together, such as painting or pottery. Another fun idea is to have a themed night (see page 152). Whatever you choose, make sure it's something you both enjoy, and make it memorable.

CHAPTER 14

PESTS, INSECTS AND BUGS

Are there extra guests in your home that you didn't invite? Household pests, insects and bugs can be a real nuisance, am I right? Not all insects are bad, of course, and they're essential to maintain the natural environment, pollinate our plants and keep the food chain in check, but that doesn't mean we want them inside our homes, and some pests, such as flies and cockroaches, can contaminate our food, making it unsafe for consumption. So, here are my top tips for deterring unwanted critters in your home.

No More Ants

To deter ants from entering your home, there are a few simple steps you can take. First, make sure to keep your kitchen and other food-storage areas clean and free of crumbs or spills. Wipe down counters, sweep floors regularly and store food in sealed containers. Additionally, try to eliminate any spills in your home, as ants are attracted to moisture as well as food. Finally, you can make your own ant repellent by mixing one part white vinegar and one part water with 20 drops of essential oil. Spray this mixture near doorways or other areas where ants tend to enter, or use it to wipe down surfaces in your home.

Make Mosquito Repellent

I seem to be a magnet for mosquitoes – no, really, they always bite me whenever they get the chance. It's a well-known fact that some people are more attractive to mosquitoes than others, based on factors such as genetics, body smell and even blood type. Unfortunately, I am one of those people. Yay me! Living in London, I don't get many bites, but whenever I travel, I get bitten a lot. I still remember when I went to Tunisia and came back with a mosquito bite the size of my fist. The store-bought mosquito-repellent sprays are too strong for me – they make me cough – so I have started making my own. To make a mosquito-repellent spray, I mix 60ml (¼ cup) of distilled water with 60ml (¼ cup) of witch hazel. Then, I add 10 drops of lemongrass essential oil and 10 drops of citronella essential oil. Next, I pour all of the ingredients into a small glass or plastic atomiser. Finally, I shake the mixture well and spray it liberally on myself and my surroundings to keep the mosquitoes away.

Trap Fruit Flies

Are fruit flies bothering you by hovering around your fruit, vegetables or even your bins? Unfortunately, it is a common problem in many households, especially during summer. Fruit flies tend to lay their eggs in our homes, making the infestation worse. To get rid of them, you must determine their source. Discard any open food items they're attracted to and disinfect the area. If they're hovering around the bin, remove the rubbish and wipe the bin down with disinfectant.

In some cases, removing their 'home' can be enough to drive them away. Initially, I was cynical about this trap hack, but I gave it a try and it worked like a charm. If you have vinegar and washing-up liquid (dish soap) in your cabinet, fill a small bowl or glass with them (any vinegar works), cover it with cling film and poke tiny holes in the top with a toothpick. Flies are attracted to vinegar, and once they crawl inside the holes, they won't be able to escape.

Send Cockroaches Packing

Dealing with cockroaches in your home can be distressing. They are unsanitary and potentially dangerous. Once they feel at home, it can be very difficult to get rid of them. A simple solution to repel cockroaches is to add a few drops of citrus and peppermint essential oils in a bottle of water and spray it anywhere cockroaches congregate. They dislike the smell, so it will typically make them plug their noses and run.

Fend Off Spiders

I have an intense fear of spiders. I feel like everyone says that, but arachnophobia is my middle name. If there's a spider in my home, I won't rest until it's been evicted. Poor Konan, the number of times he's had to come to my rescue because of this. I know spiders pose no harm in the home; in fact, they help control the number of other bugs and even other spiders. Hey, what I don't see won't hurt me. But the moment I see a new eight-legged friend, I don't want them around me. Fortunately, there are natural spider deterrents that can keep them away without causing them any harm. For instance, spiders dislike the smell of peppermint, so you can make a spray by mixing 200ml (¾ cup) of water with 10 to 15 drops of peppermint essential oil and spraying it in areas where spiders tend to hide. You can also place cotton balls with a few drops of peppermint oil in strategic spots around your home. Additionally, cinnamon has a scent that spiders dislike, so you can place cinnamon sticks, powder or fragrance oils in areas where spiders might enter, such as basements, attics, windowsills and door frames.

Goodbye, Bed Bugs

Do you remember your parent or guardian tucking you in at night and whispering the famous bedtime rhyme 'Good night! Sleep tight! Don't let the bed bugs bite'? Well, it turns out, those bed bugs are no joke! They are real-life critters that feast on you while you're trying to catch some sleep. Who knew bedtime could be so dangerous? But don't worry, there is a way to stop those creepy crawlers keeping you up at night. To create a spray that gets rid of bed bugs, mix 200ml (¾ cup) of water with 15 drops of lavender oil and 15 drops of peppermint oil. First, remove all bedding, including any mattress toppers. Next, spray the solution onto the bare mattress until it is completely soaked. Then, spray the bedding and run it through a hot cycle of at least 50°C. Allow everything to dry completely before using a vacuum to remove any dead bed bugs. Be sure to empty your vacuum immediately.

CHAPTER 15

GARDENING HACKS

As a new plant mum, I have recently taken on the responsibility of caring for my first indoor and outdoor garden. Being a novice, I am learning as I go and discovering the joys and challenges of nurturing my plants. Although I am no Alan Titchmarsh, I find it fulfilling despite the challenges. Watching my plants grow and thrive is the most rewarding part of having a garden. It's a magical feeling to see the tiny seeds I sowed sprout and develop into something beautiful and fruitful. I am constantly exploring new ways to care for my little green family. Over time, I have discovered some hacks that have worked wonders for me. I hope this collection of handy gardening hints will give you some effective new techniques to get the beautiful garden you've always wanted.

Make Your Own Compost

Plants need essential nutrients to grow and fight off harmful diseases, just like we do. The good news is that you don't have to spend a fortune on expensive fertilisers. You can make your own at home and save money. Homemade compost is an excellent natural fertiliser that is packed with beneficial nutrients for your plants. It's a sustainable solution, as you'll never run out of it as long as you have food scraps to dispose of. If you have an outdoor space, you can create your own compost pile by throwing fruit and vegetable scraps, used coffee grounds, eggshells, banana peels and tea bags into a weather- and critter-proof bin. Every two to three weeks, add a splash of water and turn the compost with a shovel. After a few months, you'll have dark, crumbly and microorganism-rich soil that your plants will love.

Use Banana Peel as Fertiliser

Bananas are rich in potassium, which is an essential nutrient that helps strengthen plant roots, build up their resistance to disease and enhance their ability to withstand drought. So, instead of throwing away your banana peels, chop them up and bury them alongside your vegetable garden. You can cover them with a thick layer of soil or use extra compost that you may have on hand. Banana peel works wonders as a homemade plant fertiliser for a variety of plants, including tomatoes, potatoes and Monsteras. Give it a try and watch your plants thrive!

TANYA'S TIP

To keep fruit flies away from your indoor plants, soak banana peels in water for up to two days, then strain the mixture. Now you have potassium-rich water that you can use to shower your plants and keep them healthy. Simply pour the water into the soil or add it to a spray bottle and spray it onto the leaves.

Make DIY Seed-starting Pots

If you're an avid gardener, you know how expensive it can be to purchase seed starter pots. But fear not, you can easily

make your own using upcycled household items. Not only is it economical, but it's also an eco-friendly way to repurpose items that might otherwise end up in the bin. Some great options for seed starter pots include empty egg cartons, cardboard toilet rolls and even pots made out of newspaper. These items work well because they are biodegradable, allowing you to plant the entire pot in the ground when the seedling is ready. With a little creativity, you can make unique and charming seed starter pots that will add a personal touch to your gardening endeavours.

Dust Seedlings with Cinnamon

Cinnamon has antifungal properties which can prevent damping-off disease, which is a common fungal disease that affects seedlings. It also contains nutrients such as potassium, phosphorus and nitrogen, which are essential for plant growth. Additionally, cinnamon can act as a natural rooting hormone, encouraging the growth of new roots in cuttings and seedlings. Simply dust a small amount of cinnamon on the soil around the base of your plants or on the seeds themselves before planting. This natural and inexpensive method can help give your plants a healthy start and promote their growth.

Prevent Root Rot

Overwatering your plants is one of the easiest ways to kill them. If the roots remain soaked in water for a long time, they can develop root rot, which can eventually kill them. Water settling at the bottom of plant pots can cause this problem. To avoid this, you can cut up old sponges and place them at the bottom of the pot. The sponges will help to retain moisture and provide necessary air space, while also preventing water from flowing out of the pot. The sponges act as a water reserve, keeping the soil moist for a longer period of time.

TANYA'S TIP

To prevent your plants from getting too much water, you can try bottom watering. This involves placing your plant in a container of water and letting the plant drink for five minutes. Remove the plant and voilà! You've watered your plant from the bottom up.

Make DIY Watering Cans

When it comes to watering your plants, it can be a hassle if you only have one watering can. Refilling it multiple times can be time-consuming and tiring. However, you don't have to spend extra money on buying more watering cans. Instead, you can repurpose old milk cartons as an alternative. All you need to do is drill a few holes in the caps (or hammer a nail all the way through), fill up the cartons with water and you're good to go. This not only saves you money, but also helps reduce waste by giving new life to an item that would otherwise have been thrown away. So, next time you run out of watering cans, give this DIY solution a try!

How to Water Your Plants While Away

Going on a holiday can be exciting, but the preparations can be overwhelming. You have to empty out the fridge, do the laundry and find someone to take care of your furry friend. But wait, what about your green babies? Don't let them wither away while you're enjoying the sun. If you can't find anyone to water them, don't worry – self-watering systems are the saviours of plant lovers who also love to travel. Here are a few hacks you can try:

- Have you ever heard of the upside-down bottle trick? It is a simple yet effective way to ensure that your plants get just the right amount of water. First, take a plastic bottle with a cap and fill it to the brim with water. Then, pierce a few holes in the cap and turn the bottle upside down. Bury the bottle about 2 inches into the soil and pierce the bottom to allow air in. As the soil dries out, water will slowly drip from the bottle and into the soil, keeping your plant hydrated.

- Another hack you can try is using string. All you need to do is put one end of the string in the plant's soil and the other end in a pot or bottle filled with water. If you have large plants, you can use two pieces of string per plant. Just ensure that the water source is placed above the plant so that the water drips down, and that the string is capable of absorbing water.

Make Natural Weed Killer

If you have young children or pets and want to avoid using harmful chemicals in your garden, consider using natural weed-control methods. While it may not be effective against deep-rooted weeds, it can easily take care of shallow-rooted ones. To create a natural weed killer, mix 1 teaspoon of washing-up liquid (dish soap), 70g (¼ cup) of salt, and 200ml (¾ cup) of white vinegar in a 250ml spray bottle. This homemade solution is inexpensive and eco-friendly.

Keep Your Garden Pest-free

Dealing with a pest infestation is undoubtedly one of the most frustrating things you can experience in your garden. If you're looking for a natural and effective way to prevent pests from infesting your garden, crushed shells could be the solution you need. Eggshells, oyster or whelk shells, for example, can be sprinkled on top of the soil that houses your plants, fruit and vegetables, creating a physical barrier that prevents these pests from laying eggs in the soil. The sharp edges of the crushed shells deter snails, slugs and bugs from crawling into the soil, effectively keeping them at bay.

CHAPTER 16

LAUNDRY HACKS

Doing laundry can often feel like an unending task, whether you're washing clothes for one person or an entire family. The sight of a large pile of laundry can be overwhelming, but once you have the basics down, it's time to take it up a notch. With the right tips and tricks, you can streamline your laundry process and ensure that your favourite outfits come out consistently clean, always smell amazing and stay in good condition. Not only will this cut down on the time you spend doing laundry, but it will also help extend the life of your clothing.

Clean Your Washing Machine

Even though a washing machine's job is to clean, it can become a breeding ground for germs and bacteria. Think about it: your washing machine works hard to keep your household in order. However, everyday items such as smelly socks, sweaty workout clothes and bed sheets can lead to a less-than-clean machine if you don't maintain it. Detergent, soap scum, fabric softener and hard water can clog the drain. I recommend cleaning your washing machine every month to keep it smelling fresh, maintain its efficiency and prolong its lifespan. It's not as difficult or time-consuming as you might think – here's how you do it.

1 Start by running an empty cycle with hot water and 250ml (1 cup) of white vinegar in the drawer, plus 200g (¾ cup) of soda crystals in the drum. Soda crystals are an inexpensive and natural multi-purpose cleaner and water softener that can prevent limescale build-up in washing machines. Using this method will help remove any residue of dirt, detergent and fabric softener from the machine's interior.

2 Once the cycle is complete, wipe the inside of the washing machine with a damp cloth and a multi-purpose cleaner. Pay special attention to the rubber seal around the door, as this is where mould and mildew tend to grow. You can use an old toothbrush to scrub any mould with vinegar.

3 Next, remove the detergent drawer and soak it in hot water and washing-up liquid (dish soap) for about 30 minutes. Scrub it with a brush to remove any build-up of detergent or fabric softener. Spray white vinegar behind the drawer and leave to sit for five minutes, then wipe away any mould and limescale.

4 Finally, clean the exterior of the washing machine with a damp cloth and a multi-purpose cleaner. Dry it thoroughly with a clean towel and don't forget to leave the door and drawer open to prevent any bad odours and mould growth.

Clean Your Washing-machine Filter

Your washing machine comes equipped with a filter that collects lint and other debris. Over time, this filter can become clogged, leading to a build-up of lint and the potential for small items such as coins, hairclips or hair to become trapped in the filter. To ensure that your washer runs safely and at peak performance, it's important to clean this filter every three months. Neglecting to do so can leave clothes dirty and smelly and, over time, can cause damage to the machine itself. Regularly cleaning the filter can help prevent clogs and ensure the smooth operation of your washing machine.

1. Start by turning off the washing machine and disconnecting the power supply. Consult the owner's manual or search online for the make and model of your washer to locate the filter. Generally, most washing-machine filters are at the bottom front exterior of the machine, behind a trap door.

2. Place a towel on the floor and a shallow container on top to catch any residual water. Locate the black drain hose by unclipping the pump cover and remove the cap from the drain hose over the container to allow water to drain. Repeat the process until all the water is drained, then replace the cap on the drain hose and put it back into position.

3. Unscrew the filter cap anti-clockwise and slide it out. Water will come out onto the towel, so be prepared. You may find obstructions in the filter, such as coins, buttons or lint build-up. Remove them and wipe the filter using a damp cloth. Ensure that the filter's housing is also clean by doing a thorough inspection.

4. Fill a sink or basin with hot water and 1 teaspoon of washing-up liquid. Soak the filter for at least 10 minutes and scrub away any debris. Once the filter is clean, return it to its position. Screw the filter cap tightly into the locked vertical position.

5 Close the trap door and ensure that it is securely clicked into position. Run a short cycle on the machine to confirm that the filter is correctly placed. If everything is working, you can resume using your washing machine.

Scan the QR code for more.

Note that some newer washing-machine models are designed with self-cleaning filters, which are located within the pump system and cannot be removed. These filters do not require manual cleaning, but it's recommended to run a cleaning cycle once a month to ensure their optimal functionality.

Washing Duvets

As a cleaning content creator, I often get asked if it's possible to wash duvets in a washing machine. The answer is not quite straightforward, as it depends on the type of filling your duvet has. Generally, duvets with synthetic fillings can be washed at home, while most feather or down duvets require dry cleaning. It's always best to check the care label of your duvet and follow the recommended washing instructions.

For synthetic duvets that can be washed at home, make sure it fits comfortably in your washing-machine drum so that it can move around freely. Wash on a normal load and dry thoroughly before using it again. On the other hand, if you have a feather or down duvet and the label allows it, you can wash it on a cold gentle cycle using a non-bio laundry detergent. It's generally recommended to wash your duvet once a year, but you may want to do it more often, depending on your preference and usage. At home, we have two duvets – a lighter one for spring and summer and a higher tog for autumn and winter. We make sure to wash our duvets at least twice a year to keep them fresh and clean.

Washing Pillows

Taking good care of your pillows can help extend their lifespan and keep you sleeping soundly. It's recommended to wash your pillows every three months to remove dead skin cells, sweat and dust mites that accumulate on them. As with duvets, before cleaning your pillows, always read the care label to ensure you are washing them correctly.

To wash your pillows, use a delicate cycle on your washing machine and normal laundry detergent. Adding white vinegar to the detergent drawer can help to deodorise and freshen up your pillows. To keep the washing machine balanced and your pillows fluffy, it's best to wash them in pairs. After washing, you can air-dry your pillows or put them in the dryer with a couple of tennis balls covered in old socks, or dryer balls. These will help to prevent your pillows from clumping unevenly and keep them fluffy and comfortable. The inner cushions of scatter cushions can also be washed just like pillows.

Cleaning Trainers

It's not uncommon for people to dispose of their trainers once they get dirty and worn out. However, given that trainers can be quite expensive and the cost of living is constantly increasing, it makes more sense to take good care of them in order to extend their lifespan and save money in the long run.

Start by removing the laces and soaking them in a strong solution of laundry whitening powder and warm water while you clean the rest of the shoe. Mix a few drops of washing-up liquid into 250ml (1 cup) of warm water and dip an old toothbrush into the solution. Use this to scrub the rubber edges, tongue and soles of the trainers to remove loose dirt. Use a toothpick to remove any dirt from the bottom of the shoe. Next, place your trainers in a mesh bag or pillowcase

to prevent them from getting damaged during the wash. Add towels or sheets to the drum too – this will help cushion the trainers and prevent excessive movement during the washing cycle. Set your washing machine on a gentle cycle and use cold water (this is important, as warm or hot water can melt any glue used in the construction of your trainers!). Avoid using bleach or fabric softeners as they may damage your trainers. Once the cycle is finished, quickly remove your sneakers from the machine and stuff them with newspaper to help them maintain their shape. Leave them to air-dry outside or in a well-ventilated area.

Note that shoes made with leather or suede cannot be washed in the machine.

Straighten Out Trainer Creases

To eliminate creases and wrinkles from the toe of your trainers, stuff them with newspaper or old socks from the heel to the toe to help maintain their shape. Make sure to pack them as tightly as possible to straighten out the creases. Then lay a damp towel or cloth over the crease and iron it using the lowest temperature setting, checking the crease at intervals to avoid damaging the shoe. Once the crease is gone, stop ironing but keep the shoes stuffed until they cool. If you don't have an iron, you can steam over the creases (you can use a clothes steamer, cleaning steamer or even the steam from a kettle for this), still using a buffer between the shoe and the steamer to prevent any damage.

Cleaning Suede Shoes

Maintaining suede can be a challenge for many people, myself included. I remember getting my first pair of suede Timberland boots for Christmas. I was ecstatic! They looked so sleek and stylish, and I couldn't wait to wear them every day. However, I soon realised how difficult they were to maintain. Despite my best efforts, they would get scuffed and stained easily. I spent hours researching how to clean and care for suede shoes. In the end, it was worth it, because I was able to extend their lifespan and keep them for longer.

When your suede shoes get stained and dirty, it may seem like a good idea to toss them into the washing machine. However, this is a big mistake. Suede shoes should never be washed in the washing machine or by hand in soap and water. This is because suede absorbs water, which can actually cause stains to set into the fabric. Instead, start with a dry toothbrush or, better yet, a suede brush, and gently brush away any dirt or grit from the surface of the shoe. Follow up with a rubber eraser and work back and forth on any marks. For stubborn stains, use a clean, dry cloth dipped lightly in white vinegar or rubbing alcohol (see page 28) to work them out.

Soften Sheets and Towels with Vinegar

There is nothing quite like the feeling of wrapping yourself in a plush, soft towel or slipping into freshly laundered sheets. The sensation is simply luxurious and makes you feel pampered. It's like giving yourself a big, fluffy hug every time you use them. We usually wash our bedding and towels on Sundays, and since discovering this particular tip, it has made all the difference. If your sheets and towels feel stiff and uncomfortable after washing, and (like many people living in small spaces) you don't have a tumble dryer, you can easily soften them up by adding half a cup of white vinegar to the fabric-softener compartment when running a cycle. This quick trick will not only add softness and brightness to your linens, but also help eliminate any lingering odours. For a pleasant scent, you can even add a few drops of your favourite essential oil, such as lavender, which is known for its sleep-enhancing properties.

How to Remove Creases Without Ironing

We've all had those frustrating mornings where it takes forever to choose an outfit, only to realise that your favourite shirt is wrinkled. And to top it off, you're already running late. But don't worry, there are a couple of hacks you can try to smooth out creases without needing to get out the ironing board.

ICE CUBES

If you have a tumble dryer, try this simple trick. All you have to do is toss three or four ice cubes into the dryer along with the wrinkled garment and let it run for about 10 minutes. As the ice cubes melt, they create moisture and steam that will help eliminate creases, leaving your clothes looking wrinkle-free.

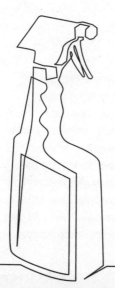

WRINKLE-RELEASE SPRAY

You can easily create your own wrinkle-release spray with a few common household items. See the recipe below:

HOW TO MAKE A WRINKLE-RELEASE SPRAY

Ingredients:
200ml (¾ cup) distilled water (boil some water, then
    wait until it cools down)
1 teaspoon of fabric softener
1 teaspoon of rubbing alcohol (see page 28)

Method: Simply combine the distilled water, fabric
softener and rubbing alcohol in an empty 250ml spray
bottle. The rubbing alcohol helps the liquid evaporate
more quickly. Shake the bottle and then spray the
solution onto your wrinkled clothes. This will help to
smooth out the wrinkles and freshen up the item too.

Prevent Sock Loss with Laundry Net Bags

I remember coming across this
meme online that said something
along the lines of, 'I am convinced
that every time a sock goes missing
from the dryer, it comes back as
an extra Tupperware lid.' It's so
relatable, as the number of socks that
vanish without a trace each year is
astonishing. Honestly, it feels like my socks
are playing hide and seek with me. Luckily, there's an
easy solution to prevent this from happening. Those mesh
bags that are typically used for washing delicates can also be
used to keep small items from going missing. Hang a large
one near your laundry basket and toss in pairs of socks as
you take them off. On laundry day, simply zip up the bag and
throw it into the wash. This simple hack will save you from the
frustration of odd sock pairs disappearing into thin air.

Dry Clothes Faster with a Towel

Another useful laundry hack is to add a clean, dry towel to the dryer with your wet clothes to speed up the drying process. The towel will absorb some of the moisture and help circulate the hot air, resulting in faster and more efficient drying. This is especially helpful if you're in a rush and need your clothes to dry quickly. Just make sure the towel you use is clean to avoid any transfer of dirt or stains onto your clothes.

Use Scent Boosters

One of my favourite laundry products is scent boosters. They are a fantastic addition to any laundry routine, as they help provide a long-lasting fragrance that keeps your clothes smelling great all day long. These scent boosters are added to your washing machine at the start of the cycle before you add your clothes. I usually add a capful of my favourite scent boosters to the drum, and my clothes come out smelling amazing every time. I highly recommend trying them out if you haven't already! I mean, who doesn't love the feeling of burying your face in a clean, freshly washed towel and inhaling that lovely scent? They come in a wide variety of scents, so you're sure to find one that you love. Give them a try and see the difference they can make in your laundry routine!

Freshen Clothes with Vodka

Did you know that vodka works as a natural deodoriser? The alcohol in it helps to eliminate odours by breaking down the bacteria that cause them. You can keep a spray bottle filled with affordable vodka and use it to freshen up your clothes before washing.

Unshrink a Jumper with Conditioner

If you've accidentally shrunk your favourite jumper and it's now too small, don't panic. There might be a way to save it! Here's what you can do: mix lukewarm water with 2 tablespoons of vinegar and 2 tablespoons of hair conditioner in a bucket. Soak your jumper in this mixture for at least 30 minutes. The vinegar will soften the fibres and the conditioner will help relax them so you can gently pull the jumper back to its original shape. After soaking, drain the liquid (but don't rinse or wring out the jumper), then stretch out the jumper carefully over a corkboard and pin it. Let it rest for an hour, then unpin, re-stretch and pin again as needed until it's stretched out to your liking. If you don't have a corkboard, you can lay it out flat on a towel and stretch it out section by section until it reaches its original shape and then let it air-dry. Keep in mind that this method works best on natural fibres such as wool, cashmere and cotton (as long as it's not felted). Synthetic fibres and blends may not respond so well to this technique.

How to Prevent Darks from Fading

Laundry detergent is great for getting rid of stubborn stains and dirt, but sometimes it can strip away colour as well. It can be a nightmare when your favourite black jeans start to fade, can't it? Fortunately, there are a few things you can do to prevent this from happening. First and foremost, separate your colours for each load and wash like colours together. To prevent the soap from causing unintended fading, turn your jeans inside out before washing them. This way, the soap strips away the wash from the inside of the jeans instead of the dark outside that you want to preserve. Lastly, adding a teaspoon of salt to the drum can also help preserve colour. Salt can set the dye and lock it in, preventing it from running in the wash and keeping it in the fabric where it belongs.

Strip Your Laundry

Every six months or so, I usually wash my bedsheets, pillows and other linens using a deep-cleaning method called laundry stripping. Over time, laundry items such as sheets, towels and bathrobes tend to accumulate residue from detergent, fabric softener, minerals in hard water and body oils. This build-up can cause clothes to look dull and fade over time. Laundry stripping is like exfoliation for your clothes, removing this build-up. It can also help lift stubborn stains and brighten clothes, making them look like new again.

To strip your laundry, you'll need a few basic tools and some common household ingredients. Start by sorting your laundry according to colour and fabric type. Wash whites, light colours and dark colours separately to prevent bleeding and fading. Fill a large bucket or bathtub with hot water, 300g (1¼ cups) of soda crystals and 600g (2 ½ cups) of laundry powder. Stir the mixture until the powders are dissolved. Add your clothes to the bucket or bathtub and make sure they are fully submerged in the water. Let them soak for several hours or overnight.

After soaking, drain the water and rinse your clothes thoroughly with clean water. During the laundry-stripping process, the water often turns dark or murky, revealing what had been lurking in your linens and other 'clean' items. It's both a little gross and oddly satisfying. Next, wash your clothes in the washing machine with 125ml (½ cup) of white vinegar. This will help remove any remaining residue and brighten your clothes. Dry your clothes as usual and enjoy the fresh, clean feeling of your newly stripped laundry.

How to Brighten Yellowed Clothes

Over time, white fabrics can lose their brightness and become discoloured, yellow, dingy or dull. Even with our best efforts to prevent dark fabric dyes from bleeding onto other items, some discoloration is almost inevitable. However, there are some measures you can take to keep whites bright. One effective solution is to use lemon juice as a natural laundry whitener and freshener. Add 250ml (1 cup) of lemon juice to the detergent compartment along with your detergent and wash as usual. For smaller items like napkins, you can prepare a solution of hot water and lemon slices on the stove. Simply fill a pot with water, add a few lemon slices, bring it to a boil, turn off the heat and add your napkins. Soak for up to an hour, then wash as usual. It's important to note that lemon juice should only be used on whites, as it can bleach certain colours. Additionally, for an extra brightening boost, you can hang your laundry in the sun for natural bleaching.

Mama's Miracle Laundry Stain Remover

My mum introduced me to this amazing laundry stain remover recipe that I've been using for a while now, and it truly is a game-changer! She reminds me of Costas 'Gus' Portokalos from *My Big Fat Greek Wedding*, who walks around with Windex® to cure everything. My mum acts like that with her magic laundry stain remover. It works on practically every kind of stain imaginable, even the tough ones like grass, grease, food, armpit stains and even blood stains! What's even better is that it uses only three ingredients that you probably already have in your cabinets, costs way less than store-bought stain remover and works like a charm! My mum got this recipe from her mama, and she passed it down to me, and I'm sure I'll be sharing it with my future children as well. But for now, it's too good not to share with you. So, here's how to make it:

HOW TO MAKE MAMA'S MIRACLE LAUNDRY STAIN REMOVER

Ingredients:
150g (¾ cup) baking soda
60ml (¼ cup) washing-up liquid (dish soap)
60ml (¼ cup) hydrogen peroxide (see page 28)

Method: Mix the baking soda, washing-up liquid (dish soap) and hydrogen peroxide in a small glass jar. Stir the ingredients together until they are combined well. The mixture should be thick. Apply a small amount of the solution directly to the stained area of the clothes. Use your fingers or a soft-bristled brush, such as an old toothbrush, to work the solution into the fabric. Let it sit for 10 minutes before washing the garment as you normally would. Store the solution in a dark cabinet or an opaque, light-excluding container because hydrogen peroxide can lose effectiveness when exposed to light.

PART 3

HOME
ORGANISATION
HACKS

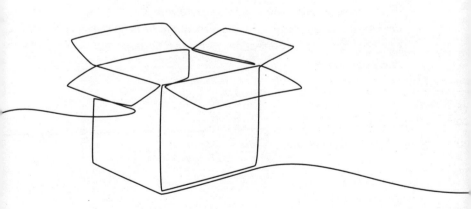

*B*ack in the day, I used to sneak into my older sister Bilo's room and spritz her expensive perfume all over me. I was such a naughty kid! Dior's Hypnotic Poison in the red bottle was my absolute favourite. I had no business wearing big girl perfume at my young age, but I couldn't resist its alluring scent. My sister would always keep her perfumes neatly lined up on her bedside table, and I would sneak in like a ninja to get my fix before heading out.

Now that I'm all grown up, I have come to appreciate my sister's impeccable organisation and tidiness. I used to envy how everything in her room was always perfectly aligned, from her make-up to her shoes to her wardrobe. But now, I understand that being organised gives you a sense of control and accomplishment in a world that can often feel chaotic.

As the professionals say, 'Tidy home, tidy mind.' If you're tired of living in a cluttered and disorganised space and want to take steps towards transforming your home into a cosy and inviting oasis, then you've come to the right place. In this section, I've compiled my essential organisation tips to help you maximise your space without sacrificing style and comfort. From clever storage solutions to space-saving hacks, you'll find everything you need to elevate your space to the next level. Remember, your home is meant to be lived in, so don't get hung up on perfection. Just take little steps and enjoy the process!

CHAPTER 17

DECLUTTERING

People who have lived in their homes for a few years can attest to the fact that there is often a large space that needs to be decluttered. This space is usually overwhelmed with possessions that are no longer needed. Examples of such spaces include the attic, garage, storage shed or, in my case, my very own version of Monica's secret closet.

I've noticed that many of my followers share my vision of having a clutter-free home or workplace but are unsure of where to begin. Not knowing how or when to start can lead to people ignoring a problem altogether, which only compounds the issue and makes it harder to tackle. To break this vicious cycle, I find it useful to divide the process into manageable stages. Decluttering can seem daunting, but you need to start somewhere. So, here are my go-to steps to getting stuck in. Let's get rid of the old and make room for the new!

Assess the Situation

It's crucial to start decluttering when you're in a positive mood. Visualise the feeling of accomplishment once a room is finished to stay motivated. First things first, take a good look around your home and identify the areas that need the most attention. Do you have clothes bursting out of your closet? Toys and games scattered around the playroom? Or maybe you're the proud owner of a 'junk drawer' that's overflowing with miscellaneous items. Whatever it may be, identify all the areas and rooms in your home that need attention so that you can focus your efforts.

Make a Plan

Now, let's create a game plan. Grab a notepad and jot down a list of the areas in your home that you plan to declutter. Creating a written plan can make the process less stressful. Not only can you tick things off as you go (there's nothing more satisfying), but it helps keep you on track. By making a list of the areas you want to declutter in your home and numbering them in order of priority, you can easily pick up where you left off when life interrupts. You don't need to be a professional organiser to get your space in order. Start by breaking down your plan into manageable steps, such as tackling one area at a time. With your plan in place, set a date to get started. And remember, prioritise progress over perfection. Don't get bogged down by the idea of achieving a perfectly organised space. It's about taking small steps to shed what you don't need and make your space work for you.

Time

My suggestion would be to begin with a small amount of time - say, 10 minutes. Taking baby steps is crucial. Although 10 minutes may not seem like much, it is a start, and you can celebrate once you've made that start! Then, add another 10 minutes the next day and another the day after that. Before you know it, you'll have cleared out an entire closet or kitchen cupboard and then half of your house, and who knows? Maybe eventually your house will be even more organised than Khloé Kardashian's pantry. You can even make it fun and create a decluttering challenge with your family or friends. Whoever declutters the most items in 10 minutes wins bragging rights and a fancy trophy (okay, maybe skip the trophy).

Get Sorting

The next step is to sort through your belongings and divide them into piles of items that you want to keep and items that you want to get rid of. Don't bite off more than you can chew. It's best to begin with a small area that you can tackle in one session, like a single drawer or your letters and paperwork. This approach will give you a sense of accomplishment and motivate you to continue with other areas of your home. I enjoy working in smaller chunks because it's more manageable and sets me up for a win. Trust me, even a few small steps can make a big difference, and remember, decluttering is a process – it won't happen overnight. Take it one step at a time and be patient with yourself. With each area you tackle, you'll feel lighter and more organised.

TANYA'S TIP

Decluttering doesn't have to be all doom and gloom. In fact, the process can be enjoyable, especially if you have helpers involved. Gather your friends, put on your favourite tunes and turn your decluttering session into a party. And don't forget to reward yourself with something sweet or a fun night out afterwards. After all, decluttering is not just about getting rid of stuff, it's also about creating space for new memories.

Donate, Sell or Throw Away

The next step in decluttering is to categorise your belongings. Once you have decided what you won't keep, sort the items into three piles: things to donate, sell or throw away. For example, you can throw away items that have expired or are broken, but you might want to sell items that are in good working condition and have some value. Making quick decisions is crucial when decluttering. If you're a hoarder, this process may be more challenging for you. I am a hoarder – I hold on to things, thinking I might need them someday. However, be strong and ask yourself if you need the item and whether it has a place in your home.

Now, it's important to follow through with disposing of the items you no longer need. You have a few options here. You can donate them to a charity shop near you, as many charities accept donations of clothes, books, electronics and other household items. Additionally, you can drop off your items at recycling banks or clothing and textile banks, which are often located in supermarket car parks. This way, you get rid of items you no longer need and contribute towards sustainable living by ensuring that these items get reused or recycled.

Local homeless shelters and women's shelters often accept donations of clothing, toiletries and household items to help people in need. Nurseries and schools may also accept donations of books, art supplies and educational toys. Animal shelters often accept donations of pet food, toys and bedding. However, it's important to check with the organisation beforehand to make sure they accept the type of items you wish to donate and to find out any specific guidelines they may have for donations.

Alternatively, if you want to earn some money, you can sell some of your items online – try eBay, Facebook Marketplace, Vinted or Depop. If the items are no longer useful, you can simply throw them away. To help you decide whether to keep, donate or sell your items, I have a flowchart. If you find it useful, you can take a photo of it!

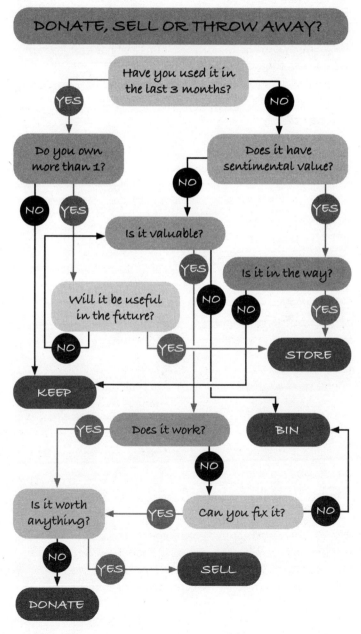

DONATE, SELL OR THROW AWAY?

Have you used it in the last 3 months?

YES — Do you own more than 1?

NO — Does it have sentimental value?

NO — Is it valuable?

YES — Is it in the way?

Do you own more than 1? NO / YES

Will it be useful in the future?

Is it valuable? YES / NO

Is it in the way? YES

Will it be useful in the future? NO / YES

STORE

KEEP

Does it work? YES / NO

BIN

Is it worth anything? — YES — Can you fix it? — NO — BIN

Can you fix it? YES

Is it worth anything? NO / YES

SELL

DONATE

Although it sounds simple enough, decluttering can be hugely overwhelming, especially if you haven't done it in a while or if there are emotional attachments to the items involved. But be honest with yourself and question if you need or use each item. If it has been sitting in a drawer or collecting dust for months or years, it's probably time to let it go. Remember, we can either have the stuff or the space – not both.

CHAPTER 18

STORAGE SOLUTIONS

Once you have finished decluttering your belongings, the next step is to organise your home to keep it neat and tidy. Many of my followers often tell me that they feel disorganised and do not know where to start with this. In such situations, I recommend creating a plan for each area of your home and prioritising the items you use the most. For example, if you have a lot of clothes, setting up a closet system is an effective way to keep them organised. It can be overwhelming to maintain an organised home, especially with children or a busy work schedule, but take your time and be patient with yourself. There is no hurry. You need not be a professional organiser to keep your home in order; we are all learning as we go. I am constantly working to improve and tweak the systems in my home to get rid of clutter and keep away as much chaos as possible! I do what works for me and am glad to share a few tips with you all.

Organise Like for Like

When I'm unsure of where to start, I resort to my trusty organiser's trick: grouping similar items together. For instance, if I were to clear out my kitchen cabinets, I would first categorise my spices, tinned foods, condiments and so on. By grouping items by type, it becomes easier to see what I possess. If I have duplicates or triplicates of items, I can remove some of the extras. If anything has expired, I can toss it in the bin. Starting here helps me understand what I'm dealing with, allowing me to select appropriate storage solutions. Additionally, I take this opportunity to determine if certain categories could be better placed elsewhere.

How to Store Items

I arrange all my belongings so that they have a designated spot, keeping similar items together. To start, I always place the items that I use most frequently in a readily accessible area. For instance, I swap out my wardrobe twice a year, keeping autumn and winter clothes out and putting spring and summer clothes in storage, and vice versa. For pet food and supplies, I suggest storing them on the lowest shelf, so they remain separate from human food. Items that are seldom used can be kept on higher shelves or in less accessible areas. You can keep your belongings in a tidy and easily accessible manner without having to purchase expensive storage bins. In my home, I often use cardboard or shoe boxes to store items and get creative by covering them with fabric to match my decor. Being organised doesn't necessarily mean spending a lot of money or buying yet more 'stuff' to put your stuff in!

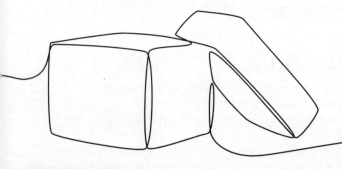

Create a System

It's a good idea to have systems in place at home to keep everything organised and running smoothly. For example, going paperless can be a great way to manage the endless stream of paperwork that comes into your home on a daily basis. To get started, try contacting your banks and bill providers to switch to paperless statements. For any other paperwork that comes in, take a photo or scan it and file it digitally. This way, you can easily reference it in the future and discard the paper originals. It's a simple solution that can make a big difference in keeping your home clutter-free.

Don't hesitate to tweak systems that are not working for you. There have been instances when I spent a lot of time setting up a system and making it look good, but when it came to daily use, it just didn't work or wasn't practical. For instance, I have deep cupboards in my kitchen, and I used to store items behind each other. It looked neat, but it was inconvenient to get the ones behind, so I ended up not using them, and they would eventually expire and get thrown out, which was a huge waste. When I realised that my system wasn't working, I organised the items on top of each other so that I could easily see and reach what I needed. It worked much better.

Use Labelling

One of my favourite ways to organise my things at home is by labelling them. This is the final touch in any organisation system, giving you a sense of satisfaction once you've purged, sorted and given everything a home. Labelling is like the cherry on top of an already good-looking cake. I label everything from my spice jars to the pantry cupboard and storage containers, especially if they're opaque, to remind me of what's inside them. Labels help not just me, but also other members of my household or guests to locate and return items to their rightful places. They can also motivate you to maintain an organised space. Drawers and even shelves can benefit from being labelled, as this not only helps you to locate things quickly, but also adds to their aesthetic appeal, giving your home-organisation efforts a polished and professional look. There are several ways to label, depending on your preference. I have a Cricut cutting machine, which I sometimes use to cut vinyl labels I've designed, and sometimes I print labels from my computer. I also use a label maker, but if you don't have access to these methods, you can simply handwrite on self-adhesive labels.

TANYA'S TIP

Along with labelling various things at home, I create a list of the contents. This helps you find things quickly, and also ensures that you don't forget about items that may be hidden away in storage. Additionally, I include a table that lists the expiry date of each item. This can be particularly handy for food items in your pantry or refrigerator, as it helps you keep track of what needs to be used up before it goes bad. By staying on top of your inventory in this way, you can save time, money and energy while keeping your home running smoothly.

My Favourite Organising Products

Here, I'm going to share with you the nifty items I find indispensable when it comes to home organisation and storage.

DRAWER DIVIDERS AND ORGANISERS

If you're looking to reorganise your home, starting with cluttered drawers is a great place to begin. You can use drawer organisers or dividers to help you separate kitchen or bedroom drawers into defined areas for specific things, instead of throwing everything into one big space. Drawers are often filled with clutter, meaning we can never find anything in them, so having dividers in there will save you annoyance and time in the long run, while utilising all the available space means you'll naturally be able to get more clutter away from surfaces. Drawer organisers will help you categorise and separate your items to keep your paperwork, stationery, clothes and accessories well-organised and easy to find. For example, you can use them to store folded socks and underwear, or belts, jewellery and hats. You can find dividers in various materials, such as wood, clear plastic or fabric, and they are available from numerous online retailers and most homeware stores.

STORAGE BOXES

One of my top recommendations for organising your home is to invest in plastic storage boxes. These offer a practical solution for storing household items, as they are waterproof and stackable, and come in various sizes. The best part is that they are clear, allowing you to see what's inside. Since many of the items stored in these boxes are not used frequently, it's easy to forget what you have in them. These boxes are perfect for large storage areas such as basements, lofts or storage units. Personally, I have found that storing craft supplies and seasonal decor (mainly Christmas bits) in several 60-litre boxes in my storage cupboard works wonders. To make things even easier, I use labels to tell me what's in each box so I can quickly locate what I need.

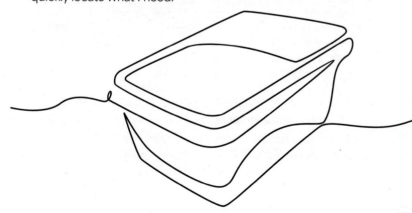

TURNTABLES/LAZY SUSANS

Turntables, also known as 'lazy Susans', are not only incredibly practical, but they also make organising your pantry, medicine cabinets or even cosmetics so much easier. They work well for containing things like oils or spices together in your kitchen cabinets, and the small ones are perfect for accessing hard-to-reach items in your refrigerator or as a place to store baking supplies in your pantry. Imagine how convenient your morning routine would be if all of your make-up and toiletries were gathered together in one place, easy to reach with one spin of a turntable.

Turntables/lazy Susans

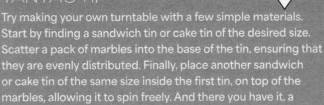

TANYA'S TIP

Try making your own turntable with a few simple materials. Start by finding a sandwich tin or cake tin of the desired size. Scatter a pack of marbles into the base of the tin, ensuring that they are evenly distributed. Finally, place another sandwich or cake tin of the same size inside the first tin, on top of the marbles, allowing it to spin freely. And there you have it, a homemade lazy Susan that's both practical and fun to use!

TIERED SHELVES

Tiered shelves are designed with multiple levels, which allow you to use height to maximise your storage space and keep everything easily accessible. They are perfect for organising items such as spices, sauces, tinned food and toiletries, with all items easily visible. These organisers are also great for arranging items in a visually appealing display.

STORAGE BASKETS

If you're looking for a storage solution that is both practical and versatile, baskets are a great option. Plus, they can be a stylish addition to any room of the house! With a wide range of styles, sizes and materials available, you can easily incorporate storage into your decor. For instance, in our living room, we use a large rattan basket to store extra blankets, which not only keeps them organised, but also adds to the room's aesthetic. We use baskets to hold and separate our cleaning supplies too, which makes these unsightly items look beautiful and makes them easily accessible. We also use baskets to store hand towels, toilet paper and other essentials on top of our kitchen and bathroom cupboards, making the most of every inch of space.

GLASS STORAGE JARS

Glass storage jars are one of my favourite things to use to organise my kitchen pantry or countertop. They are perfect for storing dry goods such as beans, rice, pasta and nuts, as well as spices, herbs and other small items. They usually have an airtight lid and silicone ring to ensure things stay fresh. The clear glass allows you to see what's inside, which saves you time when looking for ingredients. They also come in a variety of sizes, making it easy to store everything from small quantities of spices to larger amounts of flour or sugar. With these jars, you'll be able to channel your inner Marie Kondo and create a pantry that's both organised and aesthetically pleasing. Plus, if you're feeling extra fancy, you can even give them elegant labels. They really add a touch of sophistication to your kitchen or bathroom. Plus, since they are made of glass, they are easy to clean and will stay looking like new for years to come.

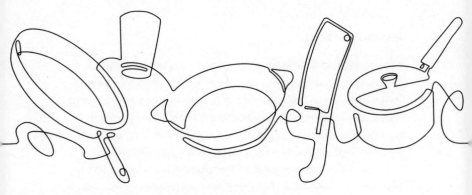

POTS AND PANS ORGANISERS

Pots and pans can be notoriously difficult to find a suitable home for, often leading to cluttered and disorganised kitchen spaces. However, investing in a pots and pans organiser can be a game-changer - it keeps your kitchen tidy and clutter-free! These racks are great for holding cookware and come with adjustable dividers and an expandable length to fit your cupboards. You can install them according to the size of your pots and pans, and they provide support and easy access to any item, making them the perfect organisational solution for bulky cookware.

MOP AND BROOM HOLDER

If you're tired of cluttered cleaning cupboards and storage areas, mop and broom holders can be a game-changer. These handy tools help you manage your cleaning supplies more efficiently while freeing up valuable floor space. You can choose from a variety of options, such as wall-mounted holders, freestanding holders and even holders that can be hung over doors. With adjustable hooks and slots, you can fit different sizes and shapes of cleaning tools into them easily. Mop and broom holders are a practical and affordable way to keep your cleaning supplies organised, accessible and free from damage. So say goodbye to the hassle of tangled brooms and mops and enjoy a more efficient cleaning experience.

POT-LID HOLDERS

A pot-lid holder is a great addition to any kitchen to keep your pot lids organised and accessible when cooking. It saves you time and space, as you no longer have to dig through a pile of lids to find the one you need. With a pot-lid holder, you can easily see which lid goes with which pot, which makes cooking a breeze. Moreover, it helps to protect your pot lids from scratches and damage, which can extend the life of your cookware. These holders can also be used to store your Tupperware lids, as they can be difficult to organise too.

How to Organise...

BOOKS

Organising books can be a daunting task, especially if you have a substantial collection. However, with a little planning and creativity, your bookshelves can be both functional and visually appealing. To begin, gather all your books in one place, then sort them by genre or category. This will help you see what you have and how much space you'll need. Next, choose how you'd like to organise them. You can alphabetise them by author or title, group them by colour, genre or arrange them by size.

Once you've chosen your method, start placing them on your bookshelves or designated area. If you have a lot of books, you may want to consider using bookends to keep them upright. You can purchase bookends in a variety of styles and colours to match your decor. Another option is to use baskets or boxes to store books that don't fit on your shelves. This works well if you have a lot of oversized books or if you want to keep certain books hidden from view. I recently stumbled upon a rotating bookcase, which is perfect for easy access and if you have limited storage. Organising your books can be a rewarding experience. By taking the time to sort and arrange them, you can create a display that makes your books easy to find and showcases your love of reading.

TANYA'S TIP

If you want to add some visual interest to your bookshelves, consider arranging your books by colour. This is more of a fun project than a necessary thing to do to keep your space tidy. If you have some extra time on your hands, you can create a rainbow effect by arranging your books in order of the colours of the rainbow. Alternatively, you can group books by shades of the same colour to create a more subtle effect.

TOILETRIES

I've experimented with a few different set-ups, but I've found that storing most of my toiletries in a cupboard under my sink works best for me. To make things even more efficient, I use stackable drawers to hold all of my items. This saves me the trouble of rummaging through boxes and cupboards, and I make sure to label everything for easy access.

GAMES AND TOYS

When it comes to organising toys and games at home, it's important to have a system that works for you and your family. One way to start is by sorting toys by category, such as building blocks, dolls and cars. Then, designate specific storage areas or containers for each category. This can help make it easier for children to find and put away toys. Consider using clear bins or labelled baskets for easy identification. To maximise space, you can also use vertical storage solutions, such as bookshelves or hanging organisers. When it comes to board games, keep them together and store them in a separate area from toys. Use a shelf or cabinet to keep the game boxes organised and easily accessible.

TANYA'S TIP

To save space and protect your puzzles and board games, transfer them into individual plastic wallets. This way, you won't have to deal with bulky boxes taking up precious storage space. The wallets provide better protection for the game pieces than broken boxes and it looks neat and organised. To easily identify each game or puzzle, you can carefully cut out the front of the box and attach it to the bag along with the game instructions. This way, you will always know what is inside each wallet without having to rummage through them.

CLOTHES

Organising clothes at home can be an intimidating task, but it doesn't have to be. Start by decluttering your wardrobe and getting rid of any clothes that you no longer wear or that don't fit (see page 190). Once you have narrowed down your collection, sort your items by category, such as shirts, trousers, dresses, etc. Next, invest in some good-quality hangers and organisers to make the most of your wardrobe space. You can also use dividers to keep your drawers tidy. It can be helpful to colour-code your clothing or to arrange them by occasion, such as work clothes or casual wear. Remember to regularly go through your clothes and donate or sell any items that you no longer wear.

TANYA'S TIP

A great way to declutter your wardrobe is to turn around your hangers. This trick helps you identify the clothes that you never wear, and which take up unnecessary wardrobe space. When you hang your clothes, place the hangers the opposite way to usual. After you wear an item of clothing, hang it back up the regular way. By the end of the year or season, donate the clothes that are still hanging backwards. This way, you'll have more space in your wardrobe and make it easier to find the clothes you actually wear.

OFFICE AND CRAFTS

Living in a one-bedroom flat in London can be challenging when it comes to having enough space. As someone who works from home, I desperately needed a dedicated office space but didn't have one. My craft supplies were also taking up space all over the flat, which made it difficult to find what I needed. After some brainstorming, Konan and I decided to turn our bedroom into an office-slash-bedroom. We rearranged some of our furniture and managed to make it work. We use a small drawers unit to hold the majority of our supplies and a monitor stand with additional drawers to hold smaller items, such as sticky notes, pens and paper clips. The rest of my craft supplies are stored neatly in my storage cupboard. Now, I'm much more organised, and my workday is more productive.

Maximising Your Storage Space

If you are struggling with storage space at home, whether it's due to living in a small house or having a growing family, it's important to remember that sometimes it has to get worse before it gets better. This is particularly true when it comes to storage. It can often feel like the space is getting smaller and smaller, but starting with a blank slate by clearing out everything can help you see what you have (see Chapter 17: Decluttering). This will help you assess your storage needs and make the most of the space available.

If you ever feel overwhelmed, it's okay to take a break and step away. Sometimes all you need is a moment to pause and relax, and something as simple as a cup of tea can make a big difference. Here are a few ways you can create more storage at home.

GO VERTICAL

If you're looking for ways to maximise storage space in
your home, then using vertical space is an excellent option.
Try installing tall bookshelves or cabinets that reach all the
way up to the ceiling. This will help you make use of space
that is often left unused. You could also use a ladder shelf;
they are extremely stylish and useful for extra storage as well
as displaying cute decor bits. Another great idea is to use the
space underneath furniture, such as beds or sofas, to create
extra storage. This can be done by using storage containers or
baskets that fit neatly under the furniture.

You can also add floating shelves or hanging storage units to
your walls. Or install storage baskets or hooks on the walls to
hang hats, scarves and bags, or to sort books, magazines, toys
and other items. When selecting baskets or hooks, choose a
style that matches your decor with a soft colour or pattern.
By using these simple techniques, you can create more
storage space without using any additional floor space.

MAKE YOUR DOORS WORK HARD

Make use of the back of doors by adding over-the-door
organisers that can hold various items such as craft, cleaning
supplies or other small objects. For instance, hanging a shoe
rack behind the door can be a great way to store extra shoes
without having them scattered all over the room. You could
also add over-the-door hooks that can be used to hang coats,
bags, towels or bathrobes. It's a smart solution that maximises
space and keeps the area tidy.

USE SPACE–SAVING WARDROBE HANGERS

I recently discovered a set of space-saving wardrobe
hangers that I wanted to share with you. These hangers are
designed to hold multiple garments on just one hanger, both
horizontally and vertically. They're perfect for heavier items

like winter coats, suits and jeans, as well as lighter items like jumpers and shirts. Each hanger has several slots, so you can store multiple garments vertically, which helps you make the most of your wardrobe's space and keep your clothes neat and unwrinkled. What's more, these multi-functional hangers can save up to 80 per cent of your wardrobe space, so they're perfect for homes with limited space. They can help you better organise your closet, making your life easier and your mornings smoother.

CUT DOWN ON BEDDING TO REDUCE CLUTTER

Do you tend to keep extra sets of sheets? Listen, I don't mean to be a sheet-stirrer, but maybe it's time to cut that sheet out if you do. Okay, let's be serious for a moment. I used to do the same, but I realised that it can lead to unnecessary clutter. Having multiple sets of sheets means more laundry to wash and fold, and you also need storage space for the bedding you're not using. That's why I would suggest limiting your sheets to just a few sets or even just one set, if possible. If you can wash and dry your sheets quickly, then having just one set is a practical option. Speaking from personal experience, I had around 20 sets of white sheets at one time (not too adventurous, I know), which I hardly used. All of them looked similar, which was pointless. Recently, I got rid of my extra bedding, and now I only have one dark set for the time of the month and a few white ones that I've saved. Trust me, it has saved me so much space and made my life easier.

TRY A SLIM STORAGE TROLLEY

A slim storage trolley is a perfect solution if you have a gap between your stove and fridge, or between your washer and dryer. It can store a variety of items, from tinned foods to laundry detergent or cleaning supplies. It is especially useful for small spaces, and as a bonus, it has wheels for easy manoeuvring.

INVEST IN STORAGE FURNITURE

Furniture with storage built in is a great way to add space to your home without compromising on design. Multi-functional furniture with shelves and compartments incorporated, such as beds, TV units, console tables, benches and more, can help you store various items, including clothes, books, TV remotes and bedding, in a stylish way. I had a coffee table with storage built in, which was perfect for holding the TV remote, extra blankets and games. Recently, I invested in an ottoman bed, which has been a lifesaver. I store my clothes, shoes and extra bedding in the storage compartment, and there's still so much room left over. If an ottoman bed doesn't suit your needs, you can also find beds with pull-out drawers. When shopping for furniture, consider units with drawers, cabinets or shelves. You can find so many beautiful options to suit your individual style, and if you're struggling for extra space, they are definitely worth the investment.

CHAPTER 19

FRIDGE ORGANISATION

Don't you just love how Pinterest can make you feel both inspired and inadequate at the same time? I came across 'fridge goals' on Pinterest and was amazed at how perfect people's fridges looked. They were so tidy and clean, and the fact that everything was organised made the food look more appetising. I took inspiration from all the pins I saw and decided to give my fridge a complete makeover. It turned out really well, but I must admit that keeping it that way is a whole different story. It takes some serious discipline to keep everything in its proper place, but it's definitely worth the effort.

My Fridge Guide

Some of my most popular videos are my fridge-organisation videos, which have amassed millions of views. It seems like you all love fridge goals just as much as I do. So, here are some tips on how to organise your fridge like a pro:

- **Fridge containers:** To keep my fridge organised, I use fridge containers. While most fridges come with drawers for fruit and vegetables, you can always buy more containers. It's a good idea to group certain items together so you can easily locate them.

- **Labels:** I have seen people label their fridge containers, and it's a great idea. Labelling makes it easier for you and everyone in your household to know where everything is, helping you find things quickly, especially during late-night fridge raids. You can even label your fridge shelves and doors if you can't label your storage containers.

- **Dividers:** In my fridge, I also use dividers in the fruit and veg drawers to separate all the fruit and vegetables. This makes everything visible and accessible, and minimises waste.

- **Fridge liners:** Another trick is to line your shelves with fridge liners or mats. You can cut them down to size and remove them for washing and soaking. Liners keep your shelves clean and provide added protection from spills and leaks.

- **Turntables:** To arrange your bottles and condiments, keep turntables (lazy Susans) on your shelf (see page 198). This provides easy access to many items and means you can quickly lift the turntable to clean spills and leaks.

- **Arrange:** To ensure that you consume items before they expire, place items with the earliest expiry date at the front and items with later dates at the back.

TANYA'S TIP
To eliminate unpleasant smells from your fridge, place an open box of baking soda inside to absorb the odours. Just make sure to place it somewhere where it won't be knocked over.

How to Store Food

How do you store your recently purchased groceries in your refrigerator? Do you store them wherever they fit, make space where needed or cram things so far back that you forget they are even there? Unfortunately, this is one of the biggest contributors to food waste. When we store food improperly, it spoils faster, and we end up throwing things out sooner and more often. No judgement here – we are all guilty of doing this, including me, but there is a way to help ourselves out, especially with food prices being so high right now.

It is essential to know which part of the fridge is suitable for different types of food to keep them safe for consumption, whether you work in the food industry or are just organising your ingredients at home.

TOP SHELF
THIRD COOLEST
Leftovers, ready to eat

DRINK SHELF

MIDDLE SHELF
SECOND COOLEST
Cooked meat, dairy, eggs

BOTTOM SHELF
COOLEST
Raw meat and fish

BOTTOM DRAWER
HUMID
Fruit and vegetables

DOOR
WARMEST
Condiments

To ensure the safety of your food, it is important to set your fridge temperature to 5°C (41°F) or below. Anything warmer than that increases the risk of harmful bacteria growth. Additionally, for proper cooling, air needs to circulate around your food. Therefore, avoid overcrowding or overstocking your fridge, as this can create warm spots and cool places, leading to spoilage.

TOP SHELF

— The top shelf in the fridge is reserved for storing leftover food, ready-to-eat meals, cooked meats and prepared salads. This is done to keep them away from raw foods and reduce the risk of contamination. It's important to note that such food items pose the highest risk of bacterial contamination, as they generally won't be cooked before consumption.

— Ensure that leftovers are covered and stored in the fridge within two hours of cooking. Avoid putting hot food directly in the fridge as it can raise the temperature inside and affect other foods.

— To make it easier to identify and consume them sooner, store leftovers in a clear container and consume them within four days.

MIDDLE SHELVES

— It's recommended to keep similar foods on the middle shelves as you do on the top shelf. These shelves are ideal for storing cooked meats, sauces or dressings, and dairy products such as cheeses, butter, cream, yoghurts, desserts and eggs. Again, ensure that all items are properly sealed before storing them on the middle shelves.

- Avoid storing milk or quick-to-expire perishables on the fridge doors where the temperature can fluctuate. Instead, store milk in the safe zone in the middle. However, you can store softer dairy products on the door shelves.

BOTTOM SHELF

- When it comes to storing food in the fridge, it is important to remember that the bottom shelf is the coldest area. This makes it perfect for raw meat and fish, which need to be cooked at high temperatures.

- To minimise the risk of contamination, wrap the meat products properly and avoid drips that could contaminate food on other shelves. Be sure to read the instructions to determine how long you can store the raw meat in the fridge before cooking, otherwise, store it in the freezer.

DRAWERS

- Although not a feature of all refrigerators, many models have humidity drawers, sometimes called crisper drawers, located at the bottom of the refrigerator, which provide a more humid environment than the rest of the refrigerator. Most drawers have a control setting that allows you to adjust between high and low humidity. If your drawers don't have any controls, they are simply high-humidity drawers. The purpose of the humidity drawer is to ensure that fresh fruit and vegetables are stored under the most favourable conditions. Fruit and vegetables tend to spoil quickly in the dry air of a refrigerator. Therefore, the drawer helps maintain optimal humidity levels, which in turn helps to keep your fruit and vegetables fresh for longer periods of time if used correctly. (To learn how to store fruit and vegetables correctly, see page 235.)

- In some cases, people may opt to store raw meat in their fridge drawers, especially if they have a limited quantity compared to their fruit and vegetables. While this is acceptable for small fridges at home, it is recommended to store raw meat on the bottom shelf for larger fridges in commercial environments.

FRIDGE-DOOR SHELVES

- The refrigerator door is the warmest part of your fridge and is opened frequently, causing temperature fluctuations. To make the most of this space, store foods that contain natural preservatives, such as juices, mayonnaise, ketchup, jam and other condiments that come in jars or bottles. These items tend to have a longer shelf-life than other, more perishable foods. You can also store fridge-safe beauty products and medication in the fridge door.

- It's important to keep the fridge door closed as much as possible to prevent the temperature from rising. Avoid storing quick-to-expire perishables in the fridge door to keep your food fresh and safe.

CHAPTER 20

HOLIDAY PACKING

Travelling is one of my favourite things to do, as it allows me to broaden my perspective and immerse myself in new cultures. Especially now that I'm working from home, I feel the need to take a break from my routine at home and go on holiday to truly unwind and relax. I've been on many unforgettable trips over the years with my family, friends and partner. So far, I've been fortunate enough to explore about 20 countries across Europe, Africa, the Caribbean and North America, but my ultimate goal is to visit all seven continents. Because, let's face it, life is too short to stay in one place. Each destination I've been to has offered a unique experience that has left me eager to discover more of what the world has to offer.

However, as much as I love travelling, I used to dread the packing process. Trying to cram all my cute outfits into one suitcase while ensuring they didn't get wrinkled was a constant nightmare. On top of that, I would always feel anxious about the possibility of being informed by airline staff that my suitcase was too heavy and having to pay additional fees. If this sounds all too familiar, fear not, my fellow travellers! After years of mastering the art of packing, I've learnt a few savvy tips that will make your life a lot easier. Whether you're a planner who packs a week ahead of time or a last-minute chancer, who complains about forgetting something every year, these hacks will help you pack more efficiently and make room for all those souvenirs you'll inevitably want to bring back home. So, pack your bags, and let's hit the road!

Rolling Clothes

Rolling your clothes when packing for a holiday not only saves space; it can also help prevent wrinkles and creases in your clothing. Start by laying your clothing item flat and folding in any sleeves or wide trouser legs. Then, fold it in half once lengthways, then a second time widthways. From there, roll it tightly from the bottom to the top and place it into your suitcase. This technique makes it easier to find specific items in your bag without having to dig through everything. Plus, it keeps your clothing more organised and can help prevent them from shifting around during travel.

Use Every Inch of Space

Prepare to put your socks and underwear inside your shoes. You'll be amazed at how much extra space you can create. If your suitcase has any zipped pockets, whether inside or outside, they are perfect for storing items that you need quick or easy access to, such as medicines or face wipes.

Pack the First Outfit You Want to Wear Last

To avoid any last-minute chaos, plan your outfits in advance. For example, if you know you'll be going straight to a business meeting or an event, pack your outfit for that last in the suitcase, putting it on the top so that you won't have to rummage through everything else to find it. This approach also eliminates the stress of putting together an outfit at the last minute.

Group Outfits Together to Save Time

One trick to make your packing more efficient is to put your outfits together as complete ensembles, to save you from the dreaded 'suitcase scramble'. This means selecting a top, bottom and any accessories you plan to wear together and packing them in one place. By grouping your outfits this way, you can save valuable time getting dressed each day. No more frantically searching through your luggage for matching items. Plus, it helps you keep track of what you've packed and what you still need to wear. Additionally, it can help you save space in your luggage, which is especially useful if you're packing light. You can even try photographing your outfits as you pack them! This way, you'll have a visual record of each ensemble and can easily mix and match pieces to create new looks. So, take some time to plan your outfits in advance and pack them together for a stress-free and fashionable holiday.

Decant Toiletries

If you decant your favourite products into smaller bottles, you can take 'just enough' for your trip, saving space in your luggage. Some of the products you can decant include shower gel, moisturiser or even liquid make-up. Of course, you can also purchase travel-size products from pharmacies, which often have great offers, although transferring your full-sized products into smaller containers can help you save money.

TANYA'S TIP

Here's a travel tip that can make passing through security checks a breeze: keep all liquids in containers of 100ml or less in a separate clear bag in your carry-on luggage for easy inspection. Larger containers must go in your hold luggage. Keeping liquids separate allows security personnel to quickly inspect them without having to search through your entire luggage. Plus, it helps prevent any spillages from ruining your belongings.

Packing Cubes

Packing cubes are all the rage on social media, and I'm so here for it. Ever since I started using them, I have been able to save a lot of space in my suitcase. These nifty little fabric containers are the secret to a stress-free packing experience. With packing cubes, you can separate your clothes by category and keep everything easily accessible. No more digging through your entire suitcase to find that one shirt you packed. Plus, they keep your clothes wrinkle-free and prevent them from getting mixed up during travel. If you're ready to level up your packing game, I highly recommend investing in a set of packing cubes.

Place Heavy Items at the Bottom

When packing your suitcase, keep heavier items at the bottom. This helps to distribute the weight more evenly and prevents your clothes from getting crushed or wrinkled. Heavier items, such as shoes, toiletry bags and books, should be placed at the base of your suitcase to create a stable foundation for the case and all your belongings. By following this simple tip, you can ensure that you can easily carry your suitcase without straining your back or arms.

Wear Your Heaviest Clothes on the Plane

When it comes to packing for a flight, it's important to keep in mind the weight limit for luggage imposed by airlines. To make the most of the space in your suitcase, consider wearing your heaviest and bulkiest clothes on the plane. This will not only save you from having to pay extra fees for overweight baggage, but also free up some weight in your luggage. Additionally, wearing your jacket or joggers can save space in your suitcase while also ensuring that you stay warm and cosy during the flight. However, it's recommended to dress in layers so that you can easily regulate your body temperature and stay comfortable throughout the journey.

Protect Delicate Items with Ziplock Bags

When travelling, I like to take extra care of my delicate items to avoid any damage. One way I protect them is by using plastic ziplock travel bags. These are perfect for packing your delicates, including lingerie, a silk scarf or other lightweight items. Simply place each item in a separate bag and seal it tightly. This method will protect your clothing from accidental pulls and snags, and keep it clean and organised in your luggage. Moreover, they're a sustainable solution, as you can reuse the bags for future trips.

Bring a Laundry Bag

Don't forget to pack a laundry bag in your suitcase to store dirty clothes. This will make it easier to separate them from your clean clothes, especially if you're travelling for an extended period. The laundry bag is like the unsung hero of your luggage, ensuring that your suitcase stays organised and tidy. When you get back home, just dump the contents of your laundry bag into the washing machine, and you're done! You no longer have to worry about separating, sorting or smelling your dirty clothes.

Bring a Blanket for the Plane

It's always a good idea to be prepared for the chilly temperatures on a plane, regardless of the season. Consider bringing a warm and cosy wrap that you can easily snuggle up in if the temperature drops. Having a compact blanket that can fit into your hand luggage when not in use is a great option. Not only will it keep you warm, but you can also fold it and use it as a pillow for added comfort during your flight.

Wrap Your Shoes in a Shower Cap

When packing your suitcase, a witty tip to make your life easier is to wrap your shoes in a shower cap. This ensures that the soles of your shoes don't come into contact with your clean clothes, keeping them fresh and dirt-free. It's a simple and easy way to keep your suitcase organised and your clothes clean while you travel. Plus, the shower cap can be reused on your next trip, making it an eco-friendly packing solution.

Carry a Reusable Water Bottle

When you're travelling through the airport, carrying an empty water bottle is perfectly fine. After passing through the security checkpoint, you can fill it at the airport café or water station. This way, you can stay hydrated throughout your journey without having to purchase plastic water bottles while exploring your destination. It's a cost-effective option, and an eco-friendly way to travel.

Keep Your Clothes Fresh with Dryer Sheets

If you want to keep your clothes smelling fresh while travelling, consider packing a few dryer sheets in your suitcase. You can tuck them into different compartments of your luggage to keep everything smelling great. Not only do they mask any unpleasant odours that may linger on your clothes, but they also act as a natural insect repellent, keeping bugs and pests at bay.

Organise Your Jewellery

Let's be honest, spending hours untangling jewellery isn't anyone's idea of a good time, especially when you're on holiday. So, if you're ready to accessorise without the headache, here's a clever hack: grab an empty toilet roll and loop your bracelets around it. Plus, you can even thread your necklaces through the tube itself, so you'll never have to deal with a tangled mess again.

Use a Holiday Checklist

Before you start drafting your out-of-office email, practising your poolside poses and dreaming of your 'I'm on holiday' cocktails, let's talk about what to pack. Planning ahead is crucial when it comes to packing, whether it's for a summer vacation, a winter ski trip, a honeymoon or a babymoon. Overpacking can be a hassle – the last thing you want is to struggle with a heavy suitcase at the airport or to ask strangers to help you close it.

To avoid all that, I suggest using a packing checklist. This will help you pack only the essentials and leave room for souvenirs and gifts (because, let's be real, we all need that tacky fridge magnet). A packing list will also make it easier for you when looking under your hotel bed when it's time to go home (we all do it). To help you get started, I have put together a comprehensive holiday packing list to help you pack like a boss. This list includes items you may require for your trip so you can be sure to have everything you need while still travelling light. Use my list as a guide when packing for your holiday, but of course, tailor it to suit your own needs.

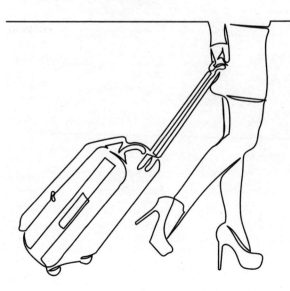

THE ULTIMATE PACKING CHECKLIST

CLOTHES

- ◯ Day outfits
- ◯ Evening outfits
- ◯ Swimwear
- ◯ Beachwear and cover-ups (sarongs, kaftans, etc.)
- ◯ Loungewear
- ◯ Nightwear
- ◯ Underwear
- ◯ Socks

ACCESSORIES

- ◯ Beach bag
- ◯ Day bag
- ◯ Night bag
- ◯ Jewellery
- ◯ Sunglasses
- ◯ Hat

TOILETRIES & COSMETICS

- ◯ Shower gel
- ◯ Wash cloth
- ◯ Body lotion
- ◯ Sunscreen
- ◯ Shampoo/conditioner
- ◯ Razor
- ◯ Perfume
- ◯ Skincare
- ◯ Make-up/make-up remover
- ◯ Toothbrush
- ◯ Toothpaste
- ◯ Deodorant
- ◯ Hairbrush
- ◯ Hair-styling products and items
- ◯ Period products

CLOTHES (OTHER)

○ Travel iron
○ Beach towel
○ Laundry bag

MISCELLANEOUS

○ Insect repellent
   (see page 162)
○ Books/e-reader
○ Waterproof phone
   case
○ Selfie stick
○ Travel pillow

ELECTRONICS

○ Camera
○ Phone charger
○ Laptop charger
○ Adaptor
○ Headphones

SHOES

○ Heels
○ Flats
○ Trainers

IMPORTANT

○ Passport
○ Money, bank card
○ Boarding pass
○ Driving licence
○ Tickets and booking info
○ Medication

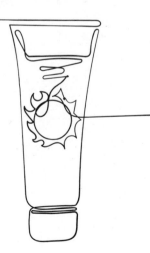

PART 4

SUSTAINABILITY
HACKS

Sustainable living is the practice of reducing your carbon footprint and living in a way that minimises your impact on the environment. This approach can also help you save money. Making small but meaningful changes to our daily habits can have a significant impact on the planet and on our wallets.

To make sustainable living more accessible, I have compiled a list of useful ideas, tips and tricks that you can implement at home to better our environment. In this section, we will explore what sustainable living means for our homes and how we can integrate eco-friendly practices into our daily lives. From reducing energy usage and waste to mindful consumption, there are many ways we can live sustainably and create a positive impact on our planet while also reducing our expenses.

CHAPTER 21

WATER-SAVING TIPS

Did you know that the average person in the UK uses around 145 litres of water per day? That's almost enough to fill two baths! Not only is this a strain on our natural resources, but it can also be expensive. However, there are plenty of simple ways to reduce your water usage and save money on your bills. Here are some tips to help you get started.

Save Water in the Kitchen

- Instead of washing dishes or vegetables under a running tap, use a bowl.

- Only run your dishwasher or washing machine when they are full, and use the eco mode if it's available. This will save you about £20 a year for each appliance.

- Make sure to use the same glass or mug throughout the day to save on extra washing up.

- Keep a bottle of tap water in the fridge, as waiting for the tap to run cold can waste more than 10 litres of water per day.

Conserve Water in the Bathroom

- Save around 10 litres of water per bath by filling the tub an inch less than usual.

- Use a timer to keep track of your shower time. Reducing the duration of your shower to 4 minutes can save you around £240 annually.

- Turn off the tap while brushing your teeth, shaving or washing. A running tap can use more than 10 litres of water per minute.

- About 30 per cent of the water you use in the bathroom comes from flushing. You can save around 20 litres of water per day by using only the small dual-flush button, if you have one.

- Fix any leaking taps. Dripping taps can waste around 90 litres of water each week, which is equivalent to a full bath!

Use Water Wisely Outdoors

- Instead of wasting leftover water from the kettle, use it to water your plants when cooled down.

- A hosepipe can consume up to 1,000 litres of water in an hour, which is more than most households use in a day. Therefore, consider purchasing a water-saving trigger for your hosepipe or using a watering can.

- Take advantage of rainy days and save up to 50 litres of water every day by using a water butt to collect water for your garden. Some water companies offer water butts at a reasonable price, starting from around £20.

- If you're washing your car, opt for a bucket and sponge instead of using a hosepipe.

CHAPTER 22

USING LESS ENERGY

Saving energy at home is not only good for the environment, but it can also save you a significant amount of money on your utility bills. By making small changes, you can make a big difference, so here are some tips on how to save energy at home.

Switch Up Your Lighting

- Switch to energy-efficient light bulbs, such as LEDs, which use less electricity and last longer.

- Turn off lights when you leave the room and make use of natural light during the day.

- Install motion-sensor lights in outdoor areas, so they only turn on when needed.

- Lampshades made from dark or thick material can dim light. Translucent shades allow your bulbs to shine brighter and are therefore more energy efficient.

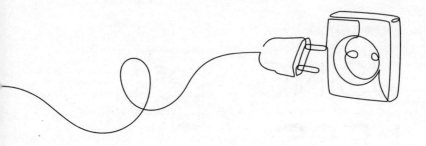

Be Smart with Appliances

- Unplug appliances when not in use, as they can still use energy even when turned off.

- Use power strips to quickly turn off multiple appliances at once.

- Choose energy-efficient appliances when purchasing new ones - look for the Energy Star label.

- Avoid overfilling the kettle, as they consume a lot of electricity. Boil only the required amount; for example, fill the kettle with only one mug of water if making a cup of tea.

- Electric cookers and microwaves consume more energy powering the clock than they do cooking. Unplug them when not in use.

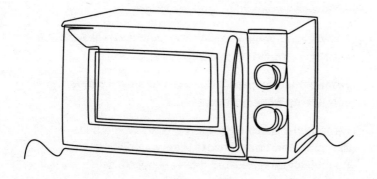

- By washing clothes in a full load at a cooler temperature (30°C), you can save a significant amount of water and electricity.

- Avoid using a tumble dryer for your clothes. Instead, dry your clothes on racks inside or outside when possible in warmer weather.

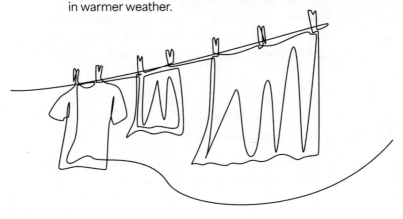

Reset Your Heating

- Lower your thermostat by a few degrees and pop on a jumper and use blankets instead, as this can save a significant amount of energy.

- Ensure that your thermostat is programmed accurately so that the heating system is activated only when you are present at home.

- Lower the temperature on radiator valves and turn off radiators in empty rooms using individual valves.

- For effective heat circulation, keep furniture and other objects away from radiators by at least a few inches.

- Lowering the flow temperature of your boiler to 55 or 60°C (130 or 140°F) can help you save a considerable amount on your gas bill.

- Laying a rug can be an effective way to increase the temperature in a room, as rugs can help insulate the floor and prevent heat loss.

- By doubling up your curtains or using heavier ones, you can reduce heat loss through windows by 40 per cent.

- Insulate your home properly, as this can significantly reduce the amount of heat lost - some councils in the UK offer this service free of charge, so it's worth looking into.

- Use draft excluders on doors and windows to prevent cold air from entering your home and to keep yourself warm during colder months.

- Close doors to unused rooms, so you are only heating the rooms you are using.

CHAPTER 23

PREVENTING
FOOD WASTE

It is concerning to know that one-third of all food produced globally is thrown away, and in the UK alone, about 9.52 million tonnes of food are wasted each year. This amount of food can feed over 30 million people, yet unfortunately, 8.4 million people in the UK experience hunger every day. Changing your habits so that you only purchase the amount of food you need will not only help the environment, but also lead to financial savings. The less food you waste, the more money you save. From measuring your portions to storing your fruit and veggies properly, here are some food hacks that are always useful, and will be extra helpful during the current cost-of-living crisis.

20 Tips to Reduce Food Waste

1 Only wash your fruit and vegetables when you are ready to eat them to avoid creating a favourable environment for bacteria to thrive and to prolong their shelf life.

2 Don't slice food until you're ready to consume it, unless you're freezing it. Chopped meat, veggies and fruit spoil faster than whole items.

3 Place lemons in a jar or bowl of water and store them in the fridge to extend their lifespan.

4 Keep cut herbs like basil, parsley and coriander fresh by storing them in a cup of water, as if they were flowers.

5 For herbs and salads, wrap them in a damp paper towel before storing them to prevent them from drying out.

6 Store delicate foods such as salads and herbs away from the back of the fridge to avoid freezing and spoilage, as the temperature at the back is often colder.

7 After cutting an avocado, to keep it from turning brown, squeeze some lemon juice on it, leave the pit inside and wrap it tightly with aluminium foil before storing it in the fridge. It may still turn brown if you leave it too long, but it will stay fresh for longer.

8 To prevent premature spoilage, store fruit and vegetables that give off ethylene gas (such as bananas, apples, avocados, tomatoes, peaches, pears and green onions) separately from ones that don't (such as potatoes, leafy greens, berries and peppers).

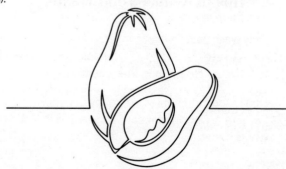

9 Keep bananas separate from other fruit and veg as they promote ripening.

10 Onions, garlic and potatoes should be stored in a cool, dark place such as a pantry or a low drawer. Keep onions and potatoes separate to prevent sprouting.

11 To allow tomatoes, mangoes, apples and kiwis to ripen properly, keep them loosely on the counter away from sunlight, heat and moisture. Once they are ripe, store them in the refrigerator to prolong their lifespan. Remember to separate ripe from unripe fruit.

12 To measure one serving of spaghetti, you can slide the pasta through the neck of a 500ml water bottle until you reach the desired amount.

13 Measure out your servings. For example, 100g (½ cup) of uncooked rice equals one serving.

14 To keep spring onions, celery and asparagus fresh for longer, store them in a jar of water in the fridge.

15 Remember to check use-by dates and avoid consuming any food that has passed its date.

16 Best-before dates, on the other hand, are a mark of quality rather than safety, so foods past their best-before dates can still be consumed.

17 Newly purchased food should be stored at the back of the fridge, allowing you to use older food first and avoid wastage.

18 It's not recommended to store opened tins in the fridge as it can lead to chemical contamination. Instead, transfer the food to a suitable container and then chill it.

19 The safest way to defrost food is in the refrigerator, as it allows for a gradual thaw without the risk of harmful bacteria growth.

20 Freezing food as soon as possible after purchase is a great way to make it last longer and reduce food waste.

TANYA'S TIP

Did you know that you can freeze a wide variety of foods, including fruit, vegetables, meats and baked goods? Even items such as bread, bananas, milk and cheese can be frozen! Freezing your food can help prevent food waste by extending its expiration date. To ensure proper storage and avoid any confusion, be sure to label your frozen items clearly.

CHAPTER 24

REPURPOSING, REUSING AND UPCYCLING

Repurposing household items is a sustainable practice that will help you reduce household waste, and allow you to get creative with everyday objects and add a unique touch to your home decor. There are many items that you can repurpose in your home, giving them a new life and function. So, it's time to turn your trash into your treasure. Here are a few examples to get you started.

Old Jars

A simple way to repurpose old jars is to use them as storage containers for dry foods such as rice, beans or pasta. You can also use them as vases for flowers or candles, or even as containers for homemade beauty products, such as body scrubs or bath salts. The possibilities are endless!

TANYA'S TIP

To remove labels from jars, soak them in warm, soapy water for 15 minutes. You will then be able to peel away the label easily.

Dessert Pots

Small glass ramekins that originally held a dessert can be used for a variety of purposes. You can use them to store small items such as craft supplies or screws and nails. They can also be used as planters for succulents and other small plants, or as serving dishes for dips and sauces. You can even use plastic lids to seal the pots, making them perfect for storing small items on the go.

Plastic Containers

Plastic containers such as yoghurt pots or mixed-and-matched Tupperware containers can be reused as organisers for small items like craft supplies or screws and nails, or as drawer dividers. You can also use them as seedling starters (see page 166) or for storing leftovers.

Tissue Boxes

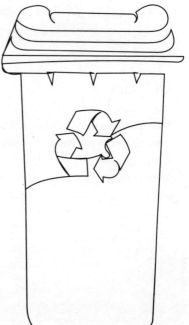

Tissue boxes can be repurposed in many creative ways. There are countless craft options, and they can serve as great storage containers. You can wrap them in paper with beautiful patterns or decorate them with ribbons or strings to create lovely containers for office supplies, recipes, seasoning packets and more.

Crockery

There are numerous ways to repurpose old cups and bowls and give them a new lease of life. You can transform them into pencil holders, planters or even candle holders. Jars can be turned into unique light fixtures by attaching them to a wooden board and putting string lights inside them. You can also paint the jars in different colours or wrap them in decorative materials such as twine or ribbon to add a personalised touch. An old dish and a wine glass can also be hot-glued together to create a beautiful cake stand or appetiser display.

Toiletry Bottles

The first suggestion is quite straightforward – consider refilling your empty toiletry bottles instead of throwing them away! If you're feeling a little more adventurous, you could cut off the tops of these bottles and paint them to create pencil holders or unbreakable vases that add a touch of elegance to your bathroom. Another innovative idea is to repurpose them into sunglasses cases.

These are just a few ideas, and I'm sure you'll come up with your own. So, next time you're about to throw something away, think twice and see if there's a way you can repurpose it instead.

GOODBYE FOR NOW

And that's it for now, my lovely readers. We have reached the end of the book, and I want to thank you all for taking the time to read it. I hope that you have learnt a little bit about me and found things that resonate with you.

Cleaning and organising can be challenging at times, especially when you feel stuck in a rut, or it seems like a chore. But I hope this book has put a little bit of fun back into it for you and helped you find inspiration.

It can be disheartening to get caught up in the perfect images often portrayed on social media. I used to compare myself to others all the time, looking at their huge luxury homes and feeling inadequate next to them. I almost didn't start my home and cleaning accounts because I thought no one would want to follow the progress of my little one-bed flat when they could swoon over all the huge homes out there. But millions of you got behind me anyway, which proves that it's not about the size of your home, but what you do with it.

What makes a home is you and your family, the love you share and the memories you create together. It's all about building a space that you love, whatever that means to you. Don't compare yourself to others, and be patient with yourself. They say Rome wasn't built in a day, and neither was your dream home.

I hope the tips, hacks and insights shared in this book have been helpful and brought you inspiration and practical solutions that you can use in your home. More than that, I hope this book has reminded you of the importance of self-care, mental health and the power of community.

Nothing brings me more joy than seeing my followers online interact and help each other in the comments. I love it when I see you supporting and uplifting each other. Let's do more of this. Life should not be about shaming and putting people down, but about having a little bit of empathy and understanding. The community we have built is amazing.

As I reflect on this journey, I am humbled by the impact that we have had together. Your stories, feedback and engagement have been the fuel that kept me going, and I am grateful for every single one of you. Thank you for being part of this journey with me. I am excited to see what the future holds for all of us, and I am grateful to have you by my side.

Before I bid you farewell, I would like to ask a favour. If you have found anything useful in this book, please share it with your family and friends. I would be thrilled to learn about any of the hacks you have tried from these pages. If you happen to post pictures or videos online while using any of the tips from this book, please tag me on @tanyahomeinspo and use the hashtag #hackyourhome, so that I can see it.

You can also follow me on @tanyahomeinspo for more hacks! You can find me on Instagram, TikTok, Facebook, Pinterest and YouTube.

Lots of love,

Tanya

ACKNOWLEDGEMENTS

I want to express a huge thank-you to all my followers who supported me throughout my journey. Your likes, shares and comments on my videos were the driving force behind my work. Your support and encouragement helped me pursue my dream and get through the difficult time of losing my dad during lockdown. This journey has been truly life-changing, and I couldn't have done it without all of you.

I am extremely grateful for my family's support. Mum, thank you for all the wonderful things you have done for me. You are the strongest and most loving person I know. Dad, I miss you every day, but I know you are watching over me, proud and smiling. To my siblings, Bilo, Rudy, Junior and Wilma, I appreciate your constant encouragement to be better and your ability to see my potential even when I can't see it myself.

I want to thank my partner, Konan, for being my rock and always being there for me. I appreciate you for being my sounding board throughout this entire process and for being my biggest supporter. You have always made me believe that I can achieve anything.

To all my wonderful friends, I feel so lucky to have such a tight-knit circle that I can count on. You've always been loyal, and I'm so grateful to have you in my corner.

I'm grateful to the amazing team at Connect for making this book possible. You've created endless opportunities for me, and I can't thank you enough.

I also want to thank my literary agent, Emily, for her dedication to this book and for connecting me to the team at HarperCollins.

Finally, thank you to my editor, Lydia, and the whole team at HarperCollins for this incredible opportunity and for believing in me.

Stay in touch

Website: www.tanyahomeinspo.com

Email: tanyahomeinspo@gmail.com

Instagram

TikTok

YouTube

Facebook

INDEX OF KEY HACKS